EDMONTON
BOOK OF
Everything

Everything you wanted to know about
Edmonton and were going to ask anyway

D1533941

MACINTYRE PURCELL PUBLISHING INC.

MacIntyre Purcell Publishing Inc.
1662-#332
Lunenburg, Nova Scotia
B0J 2C0
(902) 640-3350
www.bookofeverything.com

Cover photo courtesy of Travel Alberta
Photos: istockphoto: page 6, 8, 18, 33, 40, 60, 72, 90, 106, 128, 146, 162, 178
Cover and Design: Channel Communications Inc.

Printed and bound in Canada

Library and Archives Canada Cataloguing in Publication
The Edmonton Book of Everything /
Martha Walls.
ISBN 978-0-9738063-4-2
Edmonton (Alta.) -- Guidebooks. I. Walls, Martha, 1972 II. Title.
FC3696.18.W46 2007   971.123'34044
C2007-901784-3

Introduction

No one book could ever really be about everything, but we hope the *Edmonton Book of Everything* comes close to capturing something of the essence of Edmonton and its people. Edmonton is a fascinating city and we could have literally filled volumes. In fact, our most difficult task by far was determining not what to write about, but rather what to exclude.

The city is a fabulously diverse place with a rich and interesting history. We can claim many talents, such as W.P. Kinsella, Marshall McLuhan and Tommy Chong, as our own. We are home to the Oilers, the Eskimos and to one of the most thriving theatre scenes in the country.

This book was very much a team effort. John MacIntyre and Martha Walls were instrumental in conjuring up the concept of, and then producing, this book. A big thank you to our team of writers, researchers and editors who worked tirelessly, combing through written material, surfing the web to bring together this massive collection of facts and stories, and pouring over final drafts – Mark Wells, Tom Murray, Cheryl Mahaffy, Samantha Amara, Lynn MacIntyre and Kelly Inglis.

The *Edmonton Book of Everything* team is richer for our newfound knowledge of this city, and we hope our efforts will inform and entertain. We would like to extend a huge thank you to all those Edmontonians who shared their insight about the city for this book. The people here are, without a doubt, Edmonton's greatest attribute.

— From the editors at the *Edmonton Book of Everything*, 2007.

Table of Contents

The Land of Edmonton

Alice Major became Edmonton's first Poet Laureate in 2005. Part of her duty in this role is to write works for the people of Edmonton and to commemorate major events in the city. In 2007, she wrote the poem, "Full of noises," to celebrate Edmonton's designation as a Cultural Capital of Canada for 2007. The title draws on a passage in Shakespeare's *The Tempest*, where Caliban is describing Prospero's magic island.

FULL OF NOISES

Out of the evening dark beyond drawn blinds,
comes a low, harmonic moan — the graders
are scraping snow from ice-plated roads
and their blades send out this strange music
over the muffled blocks and rooftops
like the call of some melancholy beast
resonating in an ocean.

This city full of songs
borne on winter's airs.
Basso profundo of furnaces and motors.
The furtive percussion of crack
alley. The orange chords
of humming freeway, light's white noise.

Then the pines' tall bows strung to the tips
with the small tunes of chickadee and siskin
almost too high to hear.

We are a singing shell on an island
of white cold, an orchestra
of interlocking spheres that reaches
to the faint feet of the northern lights,

who will dance if you sing to them.
Open the curtains.

Edmonton:

A Timeline

12500 Before Present: Edmonton is a chilly and desolate place; 85 percent of Alberta is covered by glaciers.

11000 Before Present to 12000 Before Present: The first Albertans populate the area.

1670: The British Crown grants the Hudson's Bay Company (HBC) a trade monopoly in "Rupert's Land."

1690: The HBC's Henry Kelsey, with the aid of Cree guides, explores the West.

1730: The Shoshoni are the first Aboriginals of the northwestern plains to acquire horses. They get them from the Comanches to the south.

1754: The first European to visit what is now Alberta, Anthony Henday, arrives at present-day Edmonton on March 5.

1763: The Royal Proclamation assures all Natives west of the Great Lakes that their land and resources shall not be disturbed by Europeans.

1794: The HBC and the North West Fur Company establish Old Fort Edmonton and Old Fort Augustus 25 miles downstream from present day Edmonton on the Sturgeon River.

1795: The HBC establish a fur trading post at present day Edmonton.

1807: Old Forts Edmonton and Augustus are destroyed in a Blackfoot raid.

1808: Present day Edmonton becomes home to new Fort Edmonton and new Fort Augustus. Both are abandoned in 1810.

1818 -1820: A measles epidemic kills thousands of Cree.

1819: Fort Edmonton is re-established.

1821: The North West Company amalgamates with the Hudson's Bay Company; the two posts combine to become Edmonton House.

1857-1859: John Palliser, aided by Métis guide Peter Erasmus, explores the western plains. His report changes perceptions of the prairies and suggests the potential for settlement.

1869-70: Canada purchases Rupert's Land from the Hudson's Bay Company. The area, which includes much of what is now Alberta, is renamed the Northwest Territories.

1870: The bison disappear, ushering in horrific hardship for the First People.

1871: The village of Edmonton is incorporated and becomes home to a Methodist Mission on the site of the present day McDougall United Church.

Gateway to the Klondike

Beginning with the 1862 discovery of gold deposits in the North Saskatchewan River, hopeful prospectors in Edmonton tried their luck at unearthing some of the precious metal. Rewards were never great, but small amounts of gold were unearthed and the practice of "panning" the North Saskatchewan River at Edmonton continued until the early 1900s.

Although Edmonton's own waterway did not yield massive gold wealth, gold fever profoundly shaped the community. In 1898, prospectors in the Yukon discovered significant gold deposits and the Klondike Gold Rush was born. Edmonton became the start point of an "All Canadian Route" to the Klondike.

Also referred to as the "Back Door Route," the Yukon trail that started in Edmonton had several advantages. Although the route was still long and dangerous — the trek from Edmonton to the Mackenzie Delta was about 3,060 km and in good conditions would take 65 days — it also promised better weather conditions and, most importantly, it allowed gold-seekers to avoid dangerous mountain passes.

Each winter, prospector teams from around the world gathered in Edmonton. While here, prospectors outfitted their expeditions with everything from food, clothing and medicines to horses, carts, sleds and boats. Supplies for each prospector ran an estimated $270. As a result, Edmonton merchants experienced their own gold rush and items flew off store shelves.

The hotel business also boomed, providing rooms to prospectors. Not just good for the economy, the influx of Klondikers also bolstered the town's population. In 1897, Edmonton had just 1,500 residents. By the time the gold rush waned in the early 1900s, Edmonton's population mushroomed to approximately 7,000.

1872: The Dominion Lands Act is passed, offering enticing incentives — including free land — to potential settlers.

1874: The North West Mounted Police arrive in Edmonton.

1876: Edmonton establishes mail service with Fort Garry; Treaty Six is negotiated.

1877: Edmonton gets its first telegraph line.

1878: Edmonton's first post office opens.

1879: The Canadian Government's National Policy promises protective economic tariffs, a transcontinental railway and incentives for settlement in the west.

1880: The *Edmonton Bulletin*, the community's first paper, is first published.

1881: Edmonton's first public school is established.

1884: A call is made on Edmonton's first phone.

1891: The Calgary and Edmonton railway is built as far as the South Bank of the North Saskatchewan River.

1891: The first group of Ukrainian settlers reach Edmonton.

1892: Edmonton is incorporated as a town with Matthew McCauley as its first mayor.

1894: The Edmonton Thistles hockey team plays the first recorded hockey game in Edmonton.

1897: Goldseekers flood Edmonton en route to the Klondike.

1904: In October, Edmonton becomes a city, headed by its first mayor, William Short.

1904: Automobiles arrive in Edmonton.

1905: When Alberta joins Confederation on September 1, Edmonton becomes the new province's capital city.

1907: Strathcona is incorporated as a city.

Low Level Bridge

In the 1890s, as the towns of Edmonton and neighbouring Strathcona grew, businessmen in Edmonton lobbied for a bridge to span the North Saskatchewan River and join the towns. At that time, the only way to make the crossing was by ferry and these only operated when the river was ice-free.

The lobby worked and Ottawa agreed to build the bridge if the town contributed $25,000. Businessmen pooled their resources and the very day that the federal offer was made, the funds were wired to Ottawa. Construction began in 1898.

In 1899, an August flood of the North Saskatchewan forced changes to the plans and the bridge was raised an extra eight feet. In 1900, the massive undertaking was complete, the last rivet symbolically hammered in by pioneer Donald Ross. Over the years, the flooding of the North Saskatchewan has demanded the bridge be raised further.

In its 107 years, the Low Level Bridge has been a vital part of Edmonton and it has been retrofitted to allow for new modes of transportation. The first train crossed the bridge in October 1902 and the first street car in 1908. In 1949, a replica of the bridge was built to accommodate southbound traffic. In 2006, the Low Level Bridge was given a $12.7 million facelift in which sidewalks were widened and original support brackets replaced.

1908: The University of Alberta (U of A) opens its doors.

1908: Edmonton's first motion picture theatre, the Bijou, opens. Diamond Park opens as the city's first permanent baseball stadium.

1910: The Young Men's Christian Association (YMCA) opens.

1910: Edmonton's football team is officially named the Eskimos.

1912: The cities of Strathcona and Edmonton amalgamate, the same year that Edmonton's first courthouse opens.

1912: Annie Jackson joins the Edmonton Police Service, becoming the first female police officer in Canada.

1912: Cree athlete Alex Decoteau competes at the Stockholm Olympics, the only Albertan at the Games.

1913: The High Level Bridge opens.

1914: Golfers tee off at the Victoria Golf Course, Edmonton's first.

1916: Emily Murphy makes history, becoming the first woman Police Magistrate in Edmonton and in the entire British Empire.

1916: Prohibition begins in Alberta; it remains in effect for seven years.

1916: Women win the right to vote in provincial elections.

1918: The Spanish Flu epidemic kills 614 Edmontonians.

1920: A community orchestra called the Edmonton Symphony Orchestra first performs.

1921: The United Farmers of Alberta (UFA) win the provincial election and remain in power until 1935.

1922: CJCA, Edmonton's first radio station, begins broadcasting.

1923: The Grads win the World Basketball Championship.

1923: Edmontonians can light their homes using natural gas.

1925: Leona McGregor graduates with the first medical degree granted at the U of A.

1929: Emily Murphy et al. succeed in having Canadian women declared "persons" under the Canadian Constitution.

1927: Blatchford Field (City Centre Airport) becomes the first licensed municipal airport in Canada.

1929: The stock market collapses, and the Great Depression begins.

1932: Edmonton's Hunger March attracts 12,000 people before it is broken up by police.

1933: The first traffic light is installed in the city.

1938: The *Edmonton Journal* and other Alberta newspapers receive the Pulitzer Prize for opposing Alberta's 1937 Press Act.

1939: Johnny Callihoo and other Aboriginal Albertans organize the Indian Association of Alberta.

1939: King George VI and Queen Elizabeth (the Queen Mother) visit Edmonton.

1943: Social Crediter Ernest Manning becomes Premier of Alberta after the death of William Aberhart.

1947: Imperial Oil strikes oil near Edmonton, at Leduc.

1949: Edmonton's first drive-in theatre, the Starlite, opens.

1951: The *Edmonton Bulletin* ceases production after 71 years.

1953: A polio epidemic strikes Edmonton; 319 Edmontonians contract the disease and 16 die.

1954: The Canadian Football League's Edmonton Eskimos win their first of 11 Grey Cup championships.

1956: Canada's first open heart surgery is performed in Edmonton.

1960: Edmonton International Airport opens.

1969: Edmonton becomes the first Canadian city to join the North American Emergency Telephone 911 plan.

1970: Fort Edmonton Park opens.

1972: The Alberta Oilers join the Western Hockey Association. They are renamed the Edmonton Oilers in 1973.

1973-1974: An international energy crisis begins. A barrel of crude oil sells for $3 in 1973, $11 in 1974, and $39 in 1980; the price increase creates another economic boom in Edmonton.

1976: Heritage Day's is first celebrated.

1978: The *Edmonton Sun* begins publication.

1978: Edmonton plays host to the Commonwealth Games.

1979: The Edmonton Oilers join the National Hockey League.

1980: Ottawa introduces the National Energy Program and Edmonton's economy goes into a recession.

1981: Phase 1 of West Edmonton Mall opens.

1984: The Oilers win their first of five Stanley Cups to date.

1986: Three people die when the Mindbender roller coaster at West Edmonton Mall derails.

1987: A tornado levels parts of the city, killing 27.

1988: Edmonton Oiler's owner Peter Pocklington trades Wayne Gretzky to the Los Angeles Kings.

1989: Edmonton's first woman mayor, Jan Reimer, is elected.

1998: The fourth and final phase of the West Edmonton Mall, "the largest shopping centre in the world" with the "world's largest parking lot" is completed, having cost a cool $1.2 billion.

2004: On July 11, Edmonton is buffeted by the biggest rainstorm in its history, which costs the city $100 million.

2007: Premier Ralph Klein resigns. Although many agree he governed past his due date, there is suddenly a colour void in Alberta poltics.

Edmonton Essentials

Origin of Edmonton's Name: In 1794, the Hudson's Bay Company established a fort 25 km downstream of the modern city. Its name came from Edmonton, UK, the hometown of Sir James Winter Lake, then director of the Hudson's Bay Company. After several relocations, in 1808 Fort Edmonton was re-established at the site of the modern city that bears its name.

Coat of Arms: Edmonton's Coat of Arms was designated in 1994. At the top of the crest is a mace, representing Edmonton's status as Alberta's capital city. On the left is a Métis explorer, reflecting the city's fur trading past and on the right is Athena, the goddess of wisdom who represents education and the University of Alberta. These two figures, standing on green grass, are supporting a shield. The sun on the shield signifies Edmonton's above average amount of sunshine. The winged wheel on the shield represents Edmonton's aviation and industry and the sheaf of wheat, the importance of agriculture to the city's fortunes. The wave of blue across the shield symbolizes the North Saskatchewan River that runs through the city. The city motto runs across the bottom.

City motto: "Industry, Integrity, Progress."

City flag: First approved by Edmonton City Council in 1966 and updated twenty years later, Edmonton's flag includes the City Crest on a white field with two blue borders, which are the city's official corporate colours. The blue symbolizes strength and the North Saskatchewan River. The white signifies peace.

Official flower: Edmonton's official flower is the Marigold. Chosen in 1964, the bright yellow flower symbolizes sunny Alberta and Edmonton's role in the 1890s Klondike Gold Rush.

Voting age: 18

System of Measure: Metric

Incorporation: Village: 1871 Town: 1892 City: 1904

Time zone: Mountain

Area code: 780

Postal code: T5A – T6Z

Altitude: 668 m

Did you know...

that Edmonton was home to the world's largest sundae? On July 24, 1988, Edmonton's Palm Dairies concocted the 25 tonne (54,915 lb 13 oz) cool treat.

Holidays: New Year's Day (January 1), Family Day (the second Monday in February), Good Friday (the Friday before Easter), Victoria Day (the Monday before May 25), Canada Day (July 1), Labour Day (first Monday in September) and Christmas Day (December 25). Lunar New Year (Chinese/Vietnamese New Year) is well recognized in the community — although it is not a day off work. Employers may also choose to add other general holidays, such as Boxing Day or Heritage Day.

SISTER CITIES
- Harbin, Heilongjing Province, China
- Wonju, Gangwon province, South Korea
- Austin, Texas
- Nashville, Tennessee
- Hull, Quebec (now a part of Gatineau, Quebec)

PARKS
Edmonton has the longest stretch of connected urban parkland in North America and the highest per capita area of parkland of any Canadian city.
- Length of this river valley park system: 25 km
- Total area of parkland: 111 km^2
- Number of lakes within this area: 11
- Number of ravines: 14

Did you know...

that Edmonton's River Valley park system is 22 times larger than New York City's famed Central Park and eight times larger than Vancouver's Stanley Park?

> *"Edmonton is a city with a sense of possibilities, a place that is both the outpost and the threshold for great ventures . . . It is Fortress North for liberal creativity and intellectual and artistic life, the preserver of the northern vision and the northern connection for southern Canada."*
>
> **– Peter C. Newman, from Titans (1998)**

POPULATION

Edmonton is Canada's second most populous provincial capital and Canada's fifth most populous city.

- Population (2006): 712,391
- Population of Greater Metro Area (2005): 1,016,000

ALL TOGETHER

Percentage of Alberta's population falling within the Calgary-Edmonton corridor, according to Statistics Canada: 73

POPULATION IN PERSPECTIVE

With just over a million people, the population of Greater Edmonton is six times smaller than Toronto. If Edmonton were an American state it would rank 44th, just ahead of Montana and just behind Rhode Island.

Edmonton is bigger than more than 20 countries in the world, including Luxembourg and Singapore.

CRADLE TO GRAVE (2005)

- Births to Edmonton mothers: 8,575

> *"Edmonton is as big as Chicago, but it isn't all built up yet."*
>
> **– Anon. Uttered to an early 20th century American tourist who asked of the size of Edmonton.**

- Marriages: 3,868
- Deaths of Edmonton residents: 4,619

Source: Alberta Government.

LIFE EXPECTANCY
- Men: 76.2
- Women: 81

Source: City of Edmonton.

Take 5 ANNE MARQUIS' TOP FIVE ESSENTIAL READS
ABOUT EDMONTON

Anne Marquis is Acting Manager for Information Services at the Stanley A. Milner Library, situated on Sir Winston Churchill Square, in the heart of the Arts District. She shares her top five books that she feels give true insight to Edmonton and its' people. Edmonton is served by sixteen branches of the Edmonton Public Library system. Edmonton celebrated its 100th anniversary as a city in 2004 and, in honour of that birthday, the library joined forces with city archivists, educators, historians and the University of Alberta to produce the first two books on the list to celebrate and tell Edmonton's story.

1. ***Edmonton In Our Own Words*** by Linda Goyette and Carolina Jakeway Roemmich (2004).

2. ***Kidmonton: True Stories of River City Kids*** by Linda Goyette; illustrations by Robert Nichols (2004).

3. ***Edmonton: Portrait of a City*** by Dennis Person and Carin Routledge (1981): a wonderful pictorial history of the city.

4. ***The Garneau Block*** by Todd Babiak (2006): which first appeared as a serialized novel in the Edmonton Journal.

5. ***A Tourist's Guide to Glengarry*** by Ian McGillis (2002): a day in the life of nine-year old Neil, set in 1971 Edmonton.

YOU KNOW YOU'RE FROM

- You drive ten kilometres to do a five kilometre run in the River Valley.
- The biggest boat in your city is located in the biggest mall in the city.
- The second biggest boat in your city is too big for the river it's moored on.
- Your local bar owner complains that new residential development will hurt his business.
- Camping is something you do until you can find an apartment to rent.
- Your address contains the name of a hockey player.
- Your favourite summer event involves standing in a field of mud, soaked to the bone, drunk out of your mind, listening to folk music.
- You queue up for the pubs in -25 degree weather wearing short sleeves or a skirt.
- Your commuter vehicle is a pick-up truck.
- You're served a "prairie fire" on your birthday.
- Your favourite outdoor pool is on the Legislature grounds.
- You know that Calgary isn't the capital of Alberta.
- You've waited 45 minutes for a bus that comes every 15.
- Half of your football stadium is filled with Saskatchewan Roughrider fans.
- The house down the street is painted like an Edmonton Eskimos jersey.
- You go to North America's largest theatre festival for the mini doughnuts and not the acting.
- The "valley girls" are, well, homeless.
- You know what it means to "Raj against the machine."
- The longest distance you've ever walked was from the Bay to HMV and back at West Edmonton Mall.
- A night at the Commie has absolutely nothing to do with politics.

EDMONTON WHEN . . .

- The perv taking pictures of girls outdoors in bikinis is actually on assignment for the newspaper.

- Your city is home to both Guardian Angels and Hell's Angels.

- You've paid to watch a guy do push-ups outside the bar. (Go Dougie!)

- Your mayor wears an animal carcass around his neck . . . but only on special occasions.

- You step out into the -40 sunshine and say, 'Yes, but it's a dry cold."

- You use the word "Fringe" as a verb. (As in "I'm going Fringing....or "Did you Fringe yet this summer?"

- You know that Highway 2, Gateway Boulevard, the Calgary Trail, and the QEII are all the same road.

- You sneer at potholes that are less than a foot deep and less than two feet across.

- You know instantly what the acroynms WEM, NEP and LRT all stand for.

- You do a mosquito count before firing up the barbecue.

- You can golf an entire 18 holes between dessert and sundown.

- Your Shakespeare comes partly risqué with a chance of evening storms.

- You see Wayne Gretzky on ice more than 99 days of the year— or is that the Capilano Bridge.

- You've witnessed the miracle of flames being doused by oiler power.

- You don't need echinacea, or even Cold-FX, to enjoy a dry cold.

- Sourdough is a raft race and Klondike Days live the life of an ex.

- You become the cultural Capital of Canada while publishers and film crews flee to greener pastures.

- Smart growth fails to wag the sprawling dog.

THE CENTURY MARK

There are 163 Edmontonians who are 100 years old or older (as of 2005). Of these, 58 are men and 105 are women.

GIRLS AND BOYS

- the percentage of the population who are male: 49.6
- Female: 50.4

POPULATION DENSITY (PEOPLE/KM²)

Edmonton: 1067.2
Calgary: 1,279
Tokyo: 13,416
New York City: 10,194.2
Toronto: 3939.4

MARITAL STATUS (PERCENTAGE)

Never married 43.3
Married 37.4
Separated, divorced 6.7
Common-law 5.5
Widowed 4.3
Unknown 1.9
Other 0.8

Source: City of Edmonton.

Did you know...

that 17.8 percent of Edmonton's population is foreign born?

Did you know...

that in its summer 2007 edition, Edmonton was named one of Canada's top five gay-friendly cities by the magazine *Out Traveler?*

RELIGION (PERCENTAGE OF ADHERENTS)

Protestant	31.2
Catholic	29.4
Other Christian	3.9
Muslim	2.9

MAYOR STEPHEN MANDEL'S "TOP FIVE REASONS I LOVE BEING MAYOR OF EDMONTON, CANADA'S BEST CAPITAL CITY!"

Mayor Stephen Mandel is a capital-city booster who brings 30 years of business and community experience to City Hall. As President of the privately-held Mandel Group, he has been involved in business, residential and commercial real estate development, construction and hotel and sports enterprise operations. Mandel has also volunteered with the Alberta Heart Institute, Heart and Stroke Foundation, Jewish Community Centre, and Allen Gray Continuing Care Centre.

1. Sharing in the winning legacies of the Edmonton Oilers Hockey Club, the Edmonton Eskimos Football Club and the Edmonton Rush Lacrosse Team's energy and enthusiasm.

2. Meeting people from the more than 130 countries that now call Edmonton home.

3. Biking to work through our beautiful River Valley, which is 22 times larger than New York's Central Park.

4. Being a part of the visual spectacle found at any one of Edmonton's 30 year-round arts and cultural festivals.

5. The unbeatable quality of life; the 18,000 new Edmontonians moving here each year now know it too.

Christian Orthodox	2.6
Buddhist	2.1
Sikh	1.4
Hindu	1.1
No religion	24.4
Other	1.0

ETHNICITY (PERCENTAGE WHO CLAIM ETHNIC ORIGIN)

Caucasian	75.69
Asian	10.15
Aboriginal	4.62
Indian	4.24
Black	1.97
Arab	1.58
Hispanic	1.11
Other	0.64

Source: Statistics Canada.

LANGUAGES WE SPEAK

In total, there are 183,040 allophones in Edmonton (people with a language other than English or French as mother tongue.)

- Percentage whose mother tongue is English: 77.7
- Chinese (Mandarin, Cantonese, etc.): 3.6
- German: 2
- Polish: 1.2
- Phillipino: .9
- Other languages include –, Spanish, Portuguese, Ukrainian, Arabic, Dutch, Greek, Vietnamese, Cree, Inuktitut

Source: Statistics Canada.

LENGTH OF RESIDENCE

- 44.5 percent of Edmontonians have lived in the city for five years or longer.

- 12.4 have lived there three to five years.
- 22.2 percent have called the city home for one to three years.
- 17.5 percent have been mobile in the last year.
- 3.0 percent are unknown.

EDUCATION
Public schools
Edmonton has three publicly funded school districts, Edmonton Public Schools, Catholic School District and North-Central Francophone School Authority, providing kindergarten through grade 12 for our future generations.

School Numbers
- 208 schools
- 82,000 students
- 2,600 non-teaching staff
- 4,400 teaching staff

Post-Secondary Education
An estimated 170,000 students (including those enrolled at multiple schools) attend classes on several city campuses.

Post-secondary schools (full- and part-time enrollment)

Northern Alberta Institute of Technology (NAIT)	59,271
University of Alberta	47,520
Grant MacEwan College	36,342
Norquest College	6,300
Athabasca University	3,420

Did you know...

that the Greater Edmonton tourism industry hosts more than 4.4 million visitors a year?

> *"Edmontonians look down on Calgary as uncultured; Calgarians look northwards at Edmonton and dismiss it as 'Siberia with government jobs.'"*
> **– Richard Gwyn, columnist, The Toronto Star, 1 April 1978**

Concordia University College	2,346
Alberta College/The King's University College	656
Taylor University College and Seminary	470
University of Lethbridge	453
Lakeland College	151

EDUCATIONAL ATTAINMENT
- Percentage of Edmontonians with a university degree: 19.1
- Attended high school, earning no diploma: 18.7
- College certificate or diploma: 17.0
- Trades certificate or diploma: 12.5
- High school diploma: 10.7
- Some university education (but no degree): 8.0
- Attended college with no certificate or diploma: 7.4
- Less than grade nine education: 6.5

Source: Statistics Canada.

HEALTH CARE
- Number of hospitals operated by Edmonton's Capital Health in and around the city: 14
- Physicians: 2,300
- Nurses: 28,820
- Emergency visits per year: 369,000
- Hospital admissions per year: 100,000
- Health related phone calls handled per year: 400,000

Source: Edmonton.com.

They Said It

> "A fine city with too many socialists and mosquitoes. At least
> you can spray the mosquitoes."
> – **Future Alberta premier Ralph Klein in 1990, commenting on the capital
> city in his capacity as a Progressive Conservative MLA from Calgary.**

PROFESSIONAL SPORTS TEAMS

- Edmonton Oilers, NHL, 5 Stanley Cup Championships
- Edmonton Eskimos, CFL, 13 Grey Cup Championships
- Edmonton Rush, National LaCrosse League, 0 Championships
- Edmonton Cracker Cats, Northern League Baseball, 0 Championships
- Edmonton Oil Kings, Western Hockey League, 0 Championships

Weblinks

Edmonton Journal

www.canada.com/edmontonjournal/

See the local daily newspaper online – check out the day's top stories,
classifieds and education services.

University of Alberta

www.ualberta.ca

For prospective and current students, faculty, staff, alumni and donors
about faculties and departments, research, resources, services and the
university itself.

Profile of Census Tracts in Edmonton

www.statcan.ca/bsolc/english/bsolc?catno=95F0183X1996034

This profile presents data on education, income and work, families and
dwellings, as well as general population information for census tracts in
Edmonton.

Slang:

Every region and city of the world has its own distinct language. Words and expressions have been nurtured and given meaning over time. They inform the jokes we tell and provide us with a shorthand that can only come to be known by living here.

A.B.C.: Anyone But Calgary. Reflecting a long-standing rivalry with this Albertan city, this phrase is oft spouted by hockey and football fans to demonstrate their devotion to Edmonton teams, and their hatred for all teams Calgary.

AIR-1: The official name of Edmonton's police helicopter. Note the similarity to the name of the United States' presidential jet, Air Force One.

Albertabahn: The Queen Elizabeth Highway, which connects Edmonton and Calgary.

Alex, the: The Royal Alexandra Hospital, located on 111th Avenue between 102nd and 105th streets.

Avenue, the : Edmonton's busiest street-level nighttime entertainment district, Whyte Avenue, also known as 82nd Avenue.

Base, the: The Canadian Forces Base Edmonton, located just north of the city.

Big Onion, the: Another name for Edmonton, it is an obviously unfavorable comparison to New York City.

Blue and Gold: The Edmonton Oilers. The term refers to the colours of the team's home jersey, which has two colour schemes, blue and copper, and blue and silver.

Bridge, the: The High Level Bridge, the city's most prominent bridge.

Burnout: Refers either to the act of spinning a vehicle's tires on the spot, or someone who has become mentally unfit through drug or alcohol consumption.

Candy Cane Lane: This row of houses on 148th street between 100th Avenue and 92nd Avenue is well known for their elaborate Christmas decorations.

Capital Ex: A new "brand" for an old summer festival, Klondike Days, the new name reflects a celebration of city heritage with less focus on the city's indirect connection to the gold rush.

City of Champions: Edmonton's tourist moniker, which has undergone scrutiny in recent years due to the Edmonton Oilers' lack of Stanley Cup success. Perhaps it was inevitable that the City of Festivals would become its replacement.

City of Festivals: Edmonton's new official moniker.

Take 5 MICHAEL GRAVEL'S FIVE WORDS THAT DESCRIBE EDMONTON

Michael Gravel is a writer and poet living in Edmonton with his wife and stepdaughter. He writes about the city and its people. He's a founder of Edmonton's Raving Poets and is a prominent member of E-Town's poetry scene. Surprisingly, he has yet to meet Bob Dylan, and is partial to the color blue. Here he describes his take on five poetically inspired words that describe his home city.

Artistic Endeavor We love our art, our live music, our theatre, our literature. There is a festival happening nearly every day in the summer months. We've got great theatre and live music in the fall and winter. Art and festivals form the beating heart of E-Town.

Green The North Saskatchewan River valley is home to one of the largest urban park systems in North America. We love our gorgeous valley and all its recreation possibilities. After a long winter, the greening of the valley is a joy that everyone shares. Every spring it feels like getting out of jail to a field of lilacs and Mayday trees.

Stoic Getting through five months of bitter weather every year requires a stoicism that few other Canadian urban dwellers could muster. That stoicism informs every Edmontonian and makes us who we are. We're either heroic or crazy for living here. Maybe we're both.

Cold With temperatures dipping below -30c on a regular basis, E-Town in the winter is a great place to enjoy Mother Nature's full, blustery wrath.

Blue Collar We're not a white-shirts-and-ties kind of city. We're work boots and tool belts. Martinis after work? No thanks. Meet you in the pub for a pint.

"Colder than a well-digger's ass": Really cold, as in Edmonton-in-January cold.

Copper Mile: Whyte Avenue during the Stanley Cup Playoffs.

Cow Town: Calgary, Edmonton's municipal nemesis.

D.A.'s: In the 1980s a reference to the west end night-spot, Denny Andrew's American Bar, now defunct. The term refers to any new club that evokes memories of the famous D.A.'s.

Deadmonton: Slang term for Edmonton that refers to the high murder rate and the unsolved murders of sex trade workers.

Derrick: Perhaps also the name of your third cousin, in the oil biz this is the tall tower on a drilling rig.

Edmonton Block Heater: A touque.

Edmontonian: One from Edmonton.

Esks, Eskies: The Edmonton Eskimos football team.

E-town: Edmonton. Derivative of other city names that have been shortened to an initial and a tag (i.e., Toronto is referred to as "T-dot"). Popular term in rave circles due to the popularity of the drug MDMA, more commonly known as "E."

ETS: Referring to the Edmonton Transit Service, it can be pronounced "e-t-s," but also as "ets" (rhymes with "gets").

E-ville: Yes, yet another name for Edmonton.

Farmer Blow: A method of clearing one's nose without a tissue.

Fifth Street Bridge: The Walterdale Bridge.

Flat: A package of 24 cans of beer. Bottles packaged in groupings of 24 are not referred to as a flat. The word comes from the low, flat surface formed by a package of 24 beer cans.

Fort Crack: Fort McMurray. A moniker earned for the prevalence and abuse of crack cocaine in the small but booming city.

Fort Mac: Shorthand term for Fort McMurray (despite the fact that it's Fort McMurray, not Fort MacMurray).

Gooder: A worthy or notable event. For example: "When Roloson made that last minute save, that was a gooder."

Grass: Grasshopper lager, a type of beer brewed in Alberta.

Green and Gold: A popular description for the Edmonton Eskimos football team.

Gretz: A name of affection for Wayne Gretzky, who, as we all know, spent his best hockey years in Edmonton.

Hurtin' Albertan: Someone who is uncultivated.

Jasper: Short for Jasper Avenue, the main downtown strip.

K-days: Shorthand for Klondike Days, a now-dead summer celebration of the gold rush.

Kielbasa: A popular, garlicky Ukrainian sausage. Pronounced coo-ba-saw.

Ledge, Ledge grounds (or Leg): Common expression used in lieu of the Alberta Legislature building and the park area adjacent to it in downtown Edmonton.

Little India: Section of Millwoods at 34th Avenue and 94th Street dominated by East Indian businesses.

Mall, the: Unless otherwise specified, it's West Edmonton Mall, the second largest mall in North America.

Mayfair Park: The original name of Hawrelak Park. People who dislike controversial former Mayor William Hawrelak still use the old name.

Millhood: Slang term for the Millwoods neighbourhood in southeast Edmonton. The word refers to the area's reputation for gang activity and violence.

Mogas: Oil industry slang for motor gasoline.

Northside: Adjective used to describe neighbourhoods north of 105th Avenue, or residents of those neighbourhoods.

Oil, the: The Edmonton Oilers.

Oil Patch: Sweeping term for all forms of business related to Edmonton's booming oil and gas industry.

Park, the: Sherwood Park, a fast growing suburban community on Edmonton's eastern fringe.

QE2: The Queen Elizabeth II Highway, which runs from Edmonton to Calgary.

Redmonton: Political slang for Edmonton. The city contains the vast majority of the few non-Conservative ridings that exist in the province.

Rig Pig: A worker on an oil derrick.

Rocksniffer: The geologists on an oil drill site.

Rough Neck: An oil rig worker.

Sherwood Forest: Sherwood Park.

Shitty, Shithook: A u-turn.

Southside: The area of the city located south of the River Valley and associated with wealthy suburbanites.

Stroll, the: 118th Avenue, infamous for its sex trade.

Supercan: A large, pint-size can of beer.

Tallboy, tallie: A supercan.

Toolpush: The person in charge of an oil rig.

Trad: Traditional Ale, a beer brewed in Alberta.

Two-six: A 26-ounce bottle of hard liquor.

Two-fer: Two-for-one; killing two birds with one stone.

West End: Vast area of the city north of the River Valley and west of 124 Street.

Urban Geography

More than 21,000 years ago, the modern city of Edmonton was covered with a 1.5 km thick sheet of glacial ice. As these sheets melted, they formed a large glacial lake contained by walls of ice. About 12,000 years ago, this ice dam eroded and within mere days, it was gone. The water rushed out in a torrent, creating a valley called Gywnne Outlet, east of present day Leduc. It was then that the river that would be the North Saskatchewan began to wind its way through the clay earth of the region; within 3,000 years, the river we know today was created.

Animals soon inhabited the region, and were followed shortly by the humans who hunted them. At this time, the area that would one day be Edmonton was grassland. Then, 4,000 years ago, for reasons unknown, the climate cooled. No longer suitable for this grassy terrain, the grass died out and the region became a zone of parkland vegetation — an ecological designation it maintains today.

LATITUDE AND LONGITUDE

Edmonton is located at 53°32'N latitude and 113°29'W longitude. This puts the city along the same horizontal lines as Liverpool, England and Prague, Czech Republic, and along the same vertical lines as Flagstaff, Arizona, Idaho Falls, Idaho and Salt Lake City, Utah.

AREA
- Area of Edmonton: 683.88 km^2
- Area of Chicago: 606.1 km^2
- Area of Toronto: 629.91 km^2

URBAN GREEN
To preserve and beautify the city's environment, Edmonton has lined its streets and filled its parks with trees. The city has over 120,000 trees –35 percent are American elm trees, 40 percent are green ash and 15 percent are black ash. Each is worth an average $1,500 to $8,000 with larger elms being valued at nearly $55,000.

In total, Edmonton's trees are worth an estimated $870 million. Each year the city spends $2.6 million to plant between 5,000 and 10,000 trees, water 15,000 trees, inspect 350-400 trees for donation, handle 250 police reports and deal with up to 3,500 public inquiries.

Source: City of Edmonton.

EDMONTON BOASTS
- 1,879 km of local roads
- 554 km of collector roads
- 724 km of arterial roads
- 166 km of freeways
- 106 roadway bridges
- 7,400 hectares of parkland
- 1,785 sports fields
- 16 swimming pools
- 19 arenas
- 4 sports and fitness facilities

Did you know...

that although the term "buffalo" is used to describe the large mammal that once roamed Alberta, these Albertan creatures are, in fact, bison? Buffalo are native only to Africa and Asia.

- 60,000-seat Commonwealth Stadium
- 5 public golf courses
- 3 community centers
- 7 cemeteries

A River Runs Through It:
The North Saskatchewan River

The defining feature of Edmonton is the North Saskatchewan River that winds through the city. Originating in the ice fields of Banff and Jasper National Parks, this mighty river flows 1,300 km east toward the Alberta-Saskatchewan border. Before it finally empties into Hudson's Bay, the North Saskatchewan covers about 80,000 km^2 of Alberta and each year discharges more than seven billion cubic metres of water.

Long used as a travel route, first by Aboriginals and later by fur traders and European settlers, the river has been the heartbeat of the city since its founding. Although eager early 20th century gold prospectors did not find fortunes in the banks of the North Saskatchewan, the river has nevertheless been priceless to Edmonton and its people.

A 7,400-hectare series of 22 urban parks line its shores, creating an oasis of lush greenery and giving Edmonton more green space per capita than any other Canadian city. Don't let the Saskatchewan's muddy appearance fool you – this is caused by naturally occurring silt and the water of the North Saskatchewan is clean. Not just the source of the city's drinking water, it is also safely enjoyed by sports enthusiasts. With several boat launches on the city's river front, canoeists, kayakers, jet skiers and jet boaters enjoy the river, particularly in the summer months.

Fishers also play in the North Saskatchewan River Valley. The River is alive with fish, the largest and oldest species being the Lake Sturgeon. Although the average North Saskatchewan Lake Sturgeon weighs about 5 kg, fish topping the scales at more than 45 kg have been pulled from the river.

Shafraaz Kaba is a native Edmontonian. He is a partner with Manasc Isaac Architects Ltd., a founding member of the M.A.D.E. in Edmonton Society and Vice-Chair of the Edmonton Design Committee, a recently formed urban design review panel. He contributes weekly to the *Edmonton Journal* as a design columnist. Shafraaz has grown to love Edmonton winters and enjoys cycling, running, cross country skiing, skating and tobogganing in the river valley.

1. Whyte Avenue
During the day, this is Edmonton's most walkable stretch of shops, restaurants and urban delights. Spend an entire Saturday here by starting at the Old Strathcona's farmers market and making your way down the avenue with many of the turn of the century buildings still intact. By night, it is the centre of Edmonton's nightlife.

2. 124th Street and the High Street area on 102nd Avenue
The 124th Street/High Street area is catching up to Whyte Avenue as a walkable, pedestrian friendly street filled with great shops, cafes, restaurants and galleries. Boutiques and higher-end lifestyle stores make this area very livable, particularly with the character home filled Westmount neighbourhood nearby.

3. Victoria Promenade (100th Avenue between 121st Street and 116th Streets).
Stroll down this promenade for a gorgeous view of the North Saskatchewan River Valley. Benches, wide sidewalks and a

beautiful canopy encourage people to enjoy summer or winter days taking in the wide and glorious valley that is Edmonton's greatest asset.

4. **96th Street between 108th Avenue and 110th Ave.**

This under-appreciated and hidden gem is beautifully scaled and anchored by many churches. The nearby heart of Little Italy makes it a great stroll after a picnic in Giovanni Caboto Park.

5. **[A tie!] A. 112th Avenue between 64th and 66th Streets**

The seeds have been planted for a great street in this short two-block stretch with two fabulous restaurants, a retro fashion/accessories store, and a place that has delightful home accessories, not to mention a bookstore/cafe. Use this as a starting point for discovering the lovely Highlands neighbourhood and Ada Boulevard, another fantastic vantage point to see Edmonton's River Valley.

B. **Jasper Avenue & 104th Street**

Street life is returning to the main downtown drag in Edmonton with the rise of condo towers and warehouse loft conversions. 104th Street is a lovely side street which hosts the City Farmer's Market every Saturday in the summer time. New shops and cafés are emerging and are bringing back vitality and street life past office hours. Many pocket parks provide respite to the tall downtown towers.

EACH A CITY DIVIDED

To facilitate growth, in 1982 Edmonton was divided into four quadrants – northeast, northwest, southwest and southeast – that are dissected by Quadrant Ave and Meridian Street. Most of the existing city lies within the northwest quadrant.

STREETS VS. AVENUES

Since 1914, Edmonton's streets have been assigned names in a grid pattern of numbered avenues and streets. Streets run north-south and avenues run east-west. Geographically, the centre of the city is Jasper Avenue (as if Jasper was 101st Avenue) and 101st Street. Houses with odd numbers are on the east side of a street or the south side of an avenue. Technically, all street addresses are to indicate their quadrant – for example, 'NW' is added to the numbers of streets and avenues in the northwest quadrant – but as of yet, these are often omitted.

ELK ISLAND NATIONAL PARK

Although Edmonton proper is home to many a green space, just 45 km away Edmontonians can enjoy one of Canada's most impressive National Parks. Nestled in the aspen parkland (one of Canada's most endangered habitats) Elk Island National Park is home to an array of wildlife. The park is not literally an island, but the flat plains that encase the park's hills and depressions have created an enclosed sanctuary for 44 mammal species, including free roaming bison, moose, deer and elk, as well as more than 250 bird species.

The Mall

On September 15, 1981, phase one of the largest shopping mall in the world opened in Edmonton's west end. Although it would be superseded by the Mall of Americas, the Mall of Asia and the Dubai Mall, until 2004 nothing surpassed the shopping structure called West Edmonton Mall (WEM), known to Edmontonians as "the Mall" or "West Ed."

Built in three stages and completed in 1999, the WEM is the city's most famous attraction, receiving over 22 million visitors a year. Aside from the over 800 stores, there are two movie theatre complexes, two arcades, two casinos, three radio stations, a petting zoo and a dinner theatre.

There's an indoor skate park and NHL regulation-sized ice rink, a water park, Galaxyland, the Deep Sea Adventure with performing sea lions, a replica of the Santa Maria, submarine rides and a miniature golf course. WEM has a theme hotel (Fantasyland Hotel), theme areas within the mall (Bourbon Street, Europa Boulevard and Chinatown), a rock-climbing wall and the Haunted Castle and Fun House.

Its grandeur aside, the Mall has suffered its share of bad press. Animal rights activists targeted the Mall years after the deaths of three of four dolphins housed at the facility. In 2004, the sole surviving mammal was relocated to Florida. Its bird enclosures have also been criticized as birds frequently slammed into glass casings.

Other incidents have marred the Mall's image. On June 14, 1986, the Mindbender roller coaster hopped its tracks, killing three passengers and injuring a fourth. Then on Christmas Eve 2000, a drowned man was found at the bottom of the Deep Sea Adventure Lake — whether it was a case of a drunken misadventure or suicide has never been determined.

Despite these bad news stories, the Mall has been wildly successful. WEM plans to expand in the near future and who knows, it may eventually recapture its spot in the *Guinness Book of World Records* as the World's Largest Mall.

Take 5 EDMONTON'S TOP FIVE LEAST
POPULATED NEIGHBOURHOODS (POPULATION)

1. **Breckenridge Greens** (35)
2. **Meadows area** (40)
3. **Pembina** (60)
4. **Donsdale** (65)
5. **Baranow** (70)

Source: City of Edmonton.

IN THE GUTTER

Beneath Edmonton's bustling streets are a maze of pipes, gutters and waterways that make up the city's water treatment systems. The system includes:

- 1 wastewater treatment plant
- 2,083 km of storm sewers
- 1,902 km of sanitary sewers
- 937 km of combined sewers
- 17 km of foundation drains
- 61,355 manholes
- 8,565 catch basin manholes
- 49,549 catch basins
- 69 pump stations
- 55 storm water management lakes
- 52 dry ponds for storm water management
- 225 storm water outfalls
- 43 storage tanks

Source: City of Edmonton.

Did you know...

that the Greater Edmonton Area is home to 222 different neighbourhoods?

EDMONTON TRANSIT SYSTEM BY THE NUMBERS

- Number of routes: 160
- Number of bus stops (2006): 6,272
- Annual number of boarding passengers: 54.4 million

RICARDO ACUÑA'S TOP FIVE
ENVIRONMENTAL ISSUES
FACING EDMONTON

Ricardo Acuña is executive director of the Parkland Institute, a public policy research institute housed at the University of Alberta. He has been active in Edmonton's non-profit and activist communities for over 20 years.

1. The pace and extent of urban sprawl happening in Edmonton resulting in the city having one of the largest environmental footprints in North America.

2. The practice of blending sewage and storm run-off in some city pipes, and the regular practice of releasing raw sewage into the river when drainage systems are over-loaded.

3. The disappearance of prime agricultural land and important natural areas due to the accelerated development of suburbs and big-box stores on the city's outskirts.

4. The reliance on coal for the generation of the majority of Edmonton's electricity resulting in tremendous emissions of greenhouse gases.

5. The prevalence within and around the city of chemical, cement and manufacturing plants that emit toxins into the air and have the constant potential for leaks, spills and explosions.

> "Calling West Edmonton Mall a shopping centre is like calling the Hearst Castle a big house. It's an indoor circus, a combination of Rodeo Drive, Disneyland and Radio City Music Hall. You don't go there merely to shop, you go to gawk, and visitors from Houston, Texas, to Dauphin, Manitoba, can be found wandering, dazzled, through a forest of sculptures, fountains, ferns and fish . . . . The excitement is so pervasive that people often emerge, after only a few hours, dripping with sweat and complaining of headaches."
>
> **– Paul Grescoe and David Cruise, journalists, on the West Edmonton Mall in *The Money Rustlers: Self-Made Millionaires of the New West* (1986)**
>
> Source: Colombo's New Canadian Quotations

- Revenue earned in 2005: $68.2 million
- Fare: $2.50 Adult, $2.25 Youth
- Total vehicle km (2005): 37.2 million

PLAY IT AGAIN!

Edmonton has many sporting venues, events and players, all managed by the city's sports field operation team. The city offers its sports nuts:

- 120 shale ball diamonds.
- 755 standard ball diamonds.
- 840 rectangular fields
- 2,555 field fixtures
- 83 tennis courts
- 400 long jump pits
- 15 800-m running tracks

Source: City of Edmonton.

Did you know...

that about 300 million tonnes of sand and gravel were needed to build the infrastructure of contemporary Edmonton?

LET IT GROW

Edmonton has more than 30 community gardens which cover about 240,000 square feet of the city.

KEEPING IT OFF THE STREETS

In 2006, the city of Edmonton initiated the three-year Capital City Clean Up program. The program sees business and residential volunteers create squads, each led by a 'block captain.' Each squad adopts a city block to keep clean for 16 weeks.

In its first year, 533 squads kept over 2,000 blocks and hundreds of kilometers of parkland litter free. In addition to the thousands of bags of garbage collected that summer, twelve 'big bin' events –which gave people the chance to toss things otherwise too big for curbside collection — rounded up more than 6,000 junked vehicles and 770 tonnes of TVs, furniture and appliances.

FOOTPRINT

Average number of hectares used to sustain a Edmontonian (also known as 'environmental footprint,' a measure of the demands humans place on nature that shows how much biologically productive land and water each human occupies in order to produce all the resources he or she consumes and absorb all the waste he or she produces), according to a study conducted by Anielski Management and the Federation of Canadian Municipalities: 9.45

- Average number of hectares used by an Calgarian: 9.86
- Average number of hectares used by a Canadian: 7.25

Did you know...

that Edmonton's 60,000+ Elm trees is the largest concentration of disease-free elms anywhere in the world?

Take 5 FIVE THINGS YOU CAN DO FOR FREE

Get all wet at the Alberta Legislature: Believe it or not, the fountains and pools below the grand entrance to Alberta's seat of government are fair game for water play—and shriekingly popular hot spots as a result. While there, catch a free tour of the building.

Crunch & munch at a farmers market: You won't need Saturday lunch after sampling the lip-smack local fare at the bustling Old Strathcona Farmers Market, 104th Street and 83rd Avenue. Numerous other markets also beckon, including hugely popular outdoor markets in the downtown warehouse district and in nearby St. Albert.

Flip a disc at Rundle Park: Tired of paying green fees? Try disc golf at this free nine-hole course. Set in a bend of the North Saskatchewan River atop what once was the town dump, it's near a new playground, tennis courts, ball fields and riverside trails. For those whose pockets contain a few coins, there's indoor swimming and rental of roller blades, horseshoes, volleyballs, paddle boats, pedal trikes and more.

Applaud a parade: Come July 1, perch on an Old Strathcona curb to witness the mayhem of the annual Silly Summer Parade. About two week later (first Thursday of Capital Ex, the rebranded Klondike Days), cross the river to catch the summer's biggest parade. In August, watch for the Cariwest Festival, whose hugely colourful parade is a spectacle not to be missed.

Ride the North Saskatchewan: Here's a recipe sure to bust stress. Take one boat or kayak. Drive south to Devon and put in at the Lions Campground. Follow the wind of the river as far as you'd like, nudged by the current. Or, if it's excitement you're after, sign onto the Sourdough Raft Race in July, when crazily decorated boats ply the river, water weapons at the ready.

Did you know...

that West Edmonton Mall's amusement park was known as Fantasyland until a lawsuit from Disney necessitated a change to Galaxyland?

WASTING AWAY

Edmonton has been recycling household waste since 1988 and was one of North America's first municipalities to recycle milk cartons and aerosol cans. Ten years later, only 14 percent of residential waste was being recycled, the remainder ending in landfills.

The city has since improved its record. In 2002, 40 percent of the city's garbage was shipped to landfill, with ten to 15 percent being recycled and up to 50 percent being composted. Edmonton's goal is to have 70 percent of its garbage diverted from its landfills.

- In 2006 the city collected 223,061 tonnes of residential waste and 48,568 tonnes of residential recyclables.
- Of this, 34,356 tonnes was collected through the blue bag program, 7,484 tonnes from community recycling depots and 6,728 tonnes from the multi-family blue bin program.
- 88 percent of Edmontonians recycle through the blue bag program.

Source: City of Edmonton; Canada.com.

RIGHT TO THE CORE

Edmonton's downtown percolates with activity seven days a week. By mid-2006, the area was home to 60,000 workers, the place of residence of 13,000 and where 20,000 post-secondary students attended class.

The downtown wasn't always so vital. In the mid-1990s, fewer than 6,000 people lived there and office vacancy rates were high. Only in 2000 was the downtown reborn and by 2006, the city could boast the third lowest downtown office vacancy rate in the country.

Source: Edmonton.com.

1. Oliver (10,570)
2. Strathcona (5,150)
3. Garneau (4,365)
4. Downtown (4,140)
5. Inglewood (3,665)

Source: City of Edmonton.

FATHER LACOMBE CHAPEL

Edmonton's architecture is, by and large, that of a modern city. But it is also home to the oldest building in Alberta – the Father Lacombe Chapel. Built in 1861 by its namesake and aided by Métis workmen, this humble log building (part of the St. Albert Roman Catholic Mission) was built near what was then the fur trading center of Fort Edmonton. It remained a place of worship until 1870 when a new church was built, leaving the chapel to be used for storage. In 1929, the one-time chapel became the Father Lacombe Museum, and in 1977 the province of Alberta declared it a provincial historic site. In the 1980s the province acquired the historic building and moved it to its present location on Mission Hill. The Lacombe chapel has been painstakingly restored and is now open for public tours.

Did you know...

that Edmonton has over 260 hotels and motels and more than 13,000 hotel rooms?

Did you know...

that Edmonton is one of the best northern cities in which to witness the aurora borealis? This spectacular display of northern lights can be seen in the city a few times a week throughout the winter.

They Said It

"Edmonton has its mysterious ways (the avenues in my neighbourhood have sidewalks, but not the streets, so in mud or snow,
you plan your walks), and sometimes it's so plain I want to scribble all over that enormous sky. Scribble and scratch and scrawl."

– Marian Engel, author of "Life in Edmonton,"
The Globe and Mail, 24 March 1979.

THE MAC

Arguably one of Edmonton's most luxurious hotels, the Fairmont
Hotel Macdonald, or 'the Mac,' has been a seven-storey landmark on
the North Saskatchewan River since 1915. At the time costing
$2,250,000, or about $35 million in today's money, this Canadian
Pacific Hotel was built in the Chateau Style, a style reminiscent of
16th century French castles. In 1953, as the city grew, a modern sixteen storey high section featuring 300 bedrooms was added to the Mac,
to a barrage of criticism. The new design was mocked as "the Mac and
the box it came in," and was demolished in 1986.

In 1983, the dilapidated hotel closed its doors, but two years later
it was saved from demolition when it was declared a Municipal
Heritage Resource. Following several years of debate surrounding what
would be its fate, in 1988 Canadian Pacific Hotels purchased the Mac
and committed to a total restoration of the building. The Mac was
reborn, lovingly restored in all its Victorian-style opulence.

THE 'BURBS

The city has more than 20 suburban areas, many of which have recently experienced construction booms. While building permits for multi-
family units were consistent between 2004 and 2005, those issued for

Did you know...

that West Edmonton Mall was home to the world's first indoor
bungee jump?

single-family dwellings in the 'burbs in 2005 were up 32 percent over the previous year to 5,057. The areas of Terwillegar Heights, Heritage Valley and Pilot Sound received the highest number of permits at 947, 727 and 682, respectively.

Source: City of Edmonton.

AT HOME

Between 1996 and 2001, more than 25,200 new Edmonton households were formed. That increase brought the number of occupied households to over 265,000, with 59 percent being rented and 41 percent being owned. These included:

- 136,600 single detached houses (41 percent)
- 61,080 apartments, fewer than five stories (23 percent)
- 26,880 row houses (10 percent)
- 23,025 apartments, five or more stories (9 percent)
- 10,065 semi-detached houses (4 percent)
- 5,060 detached duplex apartments (2 percent)
- 2,630 moveable dwellings (1 percent)

Source: City of Edmonton.

Did you know...

that the neighbourhood of Ermineskin was named in honour of the Cree Chief who befriended well-known Catholic missionary Father Lacombe?

THIS OLD HOUSE

Percentage of Edmonton homes built before 1946: 5.1

- 1946-60: 18.2
- 1961-70: 19.1
- 1971-80: 27.6
- 1981-85: 11.6
- 1986-1990: 6.1
- 1991-1995: 6.3
- 1996-2001: 6.1

Source: Statistics Canada.

CONCENTRATION OF CHURCHES

Edmonton has over 520 places for people of all religions to worship. Many of these are found along 96th Street and 112th Avenue, an area cited as having the "highest concentration of churches" by *Ripley's Believe It or Not.*

TOUCHDOWN!

Opening its doors and runways in 1957, the Edmonton International Airport (EIA) is located in Leduc, about 30 km south of the city. Covering about 7,000 acres, EIA is the country's second largest in terms of area. Its runways can accommodate massive planes, including the Antonov — the world's largest cargo carrier and the facility has no restrictions on aircraft weight or passenger loads. Having served just over 5.2 million passengers in 2006, the EIA is the country's fifth busiest.

Source: Canadian Encyclopedia; Ottawa International Airport.

WHERE THE GRASS IS GREENER

With its 460 parks, Edmonton is one of the greenest cities in North America. There's one park for every 20 km² of land and for every 2,175 people. The 'Ribbon of Green' — a 48 km stretch along the North Saskatchewan River — alone boasts 22 major parks.

Source: City of Edmonton.

RATS!

The Norway Rat is one destructive animal. The rodents contaminate food, spread disease and their incessant tunneling can destabilize sewer and water lines, streets and even buildings. Edmonton is, therefore, blessed not to have a rat problem. This is not by luck. The province has had a strident "anti-rat" program in place for decades since rats made their debut along Alberta's eastern border in the 1950s. Strict rat control initiatives, including poisoning campaigns and public education, have succeeded. Each and every Edmontonian is responsible for keeping the nasty critters out. Under law, only research labs can have rats in Alberta and it is illegal for private citizens to keep white rats, hooded rats or any strains of domesticated Norway rats. Violators of this law face a fine of $5000.

Weblinks

Edmonton Neighbourhoods
www.foundlocally.com/edmonton/Home/Neigh-Info.htm
Want to know more about the city's many neighbourhoods? Start here!

Edmonton's Parks
www.edmonton.ca
For more information on Edmonton's 460 parks, look at this webpage maintained by the city.

ETS Trip Planner
www.edmonton.ca/portal/server.pt?space=CommunityPage&control=SetCommunity&CommunityID=238
Want to get around the city using Edmonton's Transit System? Use this handy trip planner to find your way.

Weather and Climate

Edmonton's climate is "continental." This means variable temperature ranges, low relative humidity and moderate to low amounts of precipitation.

Springtime temperatures in Edmonton range between 4-14°C. During the summer, Edmonton receives up to 17 hours of daylight a day, and enjoys average maximum temperatures in the 20-22°C range. Autumn daytime highs average at 15°C, but evenings are cool. The first permanent snow falls in early November and lingers until the end of March. Depending on wind direction, winter days can be relatively mild, at about 0°C, or downright frigid at –30°C.

MONTHLY AVERAGE TEMPERATURES (°C)

Jan	Feb	Mar	Apr	May	Jun	Jul	Aug	Sep	Oct	Nov	Dec
-13.5	-10.5	-4.5	4.3	10.4	14.1	15.9	15.1	10.1	4.3	-5.7	-11.3

Source: Environment Canada.

WEATHER AT A GLANCE

- Coldest Month: January
- Warmest Month: July
- Wettest Month: July
- Sunniest Month: July

Source: Environment Canada.

AND THE WINNER IS . . .

- Record high: 38.3°C, recorded August 5, 1998
- Record low: -49.4°C, recorded January 19, 1886
- Record wind chill: -61.1°C, recorded January 26, 1972
- Record rainfall (day): 75.6 mm, recorded July 3, 1990
- Record snowfall (day): 36.2 cm, recorded April 6, 1991
- Maximum hourly wind speed: 85 km/h, recorded October 1, 1965
- Maximum wind gust speed: 146 km/h, recorded October 1, 1965

LET THE SUN SHINE

Edmontonians soak up 2299.09 hours of sun each year, placing 12th in the country. Edmonton's sun time is not too far off the hours recorded in Canada's sunniest city, Medicine Hat, AB, which enjoys 2512.85 hours of sunshine each year.

Edmonton's sunniest season is the spring, when 687.97 hours of sun gives the city the title of 4th sunniest springtime city in all of Canada. Autumn and summer are pleasant too. In fall, Edmonton is Canada's 11th sunniest city and enjoys 452.39 hours of sun, while in summer, its 863.83 hours of sun makes it the 16th sunniest city in Canada.

GROWING SEASON

Edmonton's optimum growing season runs from May 24 — September 23. On average, Edmonton gardeners enjoy 140 frost free days a year — a full 28 more than Calgary, a city which, though 300 km south of Edmonton, sits at a higher elevation.

Did you know...

that when Edmonton's mercury hit high temperatures in 1937, city council ruled that men's bathing trunks were approved as suitable apparel for public pools?

RAIN

Edmonton receives low to moderate amounts of rainfall each year. With an annual rainfall of 365.65 mm, Edmonton is the 77th rainiest city in Canada. Edmonton's rainfall total is a far cry from the 2468.53 mm that Prince Rupert, BC receives, but is considerably more than

Take 5 FIVE THINGS TO DO IN WINTER

Cross country ski in the river valley. Outfox the lazy winter sun with an evening ski at any number of lighted and groomed river valley trails—and bless the volunteers who help make it so. Gold Bar Park is a favourite for all skill levels, but you might also try Capilano, Rundle, Goldstick, Kinsmen and Snow Valley parks. Maps available at www.edmonton.ca. (ski map).

Tempt fate on a toboggan hill. Another fine thing about a river valley: on those banks, toboggans fly. Several options dot the valley, most with run-out zones and hay bales to comfort the older set. Check www.edmonton.ca (tobogganing) for more.

Zone out at the Muttart Conservatory. On a bitter morning when even the snow squeaks in agony, the conservatory's four striking glass pyramids at 9626 96A St. offer sweet relief. Here you can migrate from steaming jungle to sun-baked desert to temperate forest to floral paradise before taking lunch in the central courtyard.

Look up! Count stars. Take advantage of the Beaver Hills Dark Sky Preserve just east of Edmonton to drink in the Milky Way and scan for Northern Lights. For a guided view of the heavens, hook up with local experts through Royal Astronomical Society of Canada (www.edmontonrasc.com) or Telus World of Science (www.odyssium.com). Gotta love those long nights.

Spend a night in Fantasyland. Okay, so you can't dream winter away, but you can spend a night in Africa or Hollywood or an Arabian dessert. Nearly there, anyway at West Edmonton Mall's Fantasyland Hotel.

1. **August 5, 1998**, 38.3°C
2. **July 14, 1961**, 35.0°C
3. **July 18, 1941**, 34.4°C
4. **June 4, 1961**, 33.9°C
5. **July 23, 1959**, 33.9°C

Whitehorse's 163.13 mm.

Edmontonians will only need to remember their umbrellas on 126 rainy days a year. In comparison, residents of rainiest Prince Rupert face an astonishing 240 wet days, and less rainy Medicine Hat just 99.

OVER THE BANKS

Every few years the North Saskatchewan River floods. In the past 150 years, this has happened more than 20 times. The greatest flood ever happened in 1915, when waters rose 12 m, spilling into Walterdale, Rossdale, Cloverdale and Riverdale, submerging these areas in a metre of water.

Since their construction in the 1960s, the Bighorn and Brazeau dams have helped regulate the flow and limit floods' severity. But still, flooding is a way of life in Edmonton and Edmontonians were tested as recently as July 2004.

Did you know...

that snowfall has been recorded in Edmonton in every month except July?

Take 5 FIVE COLDEST DAYS IN EDMONTON

1. **January 19, 1886,** -49.4°C
2. **January 26, 1972,** -48.3°C
3. **December 28, 1938,** -48.3°C
4. **February 8, 1939,** -46.1°C
5. **December 9, 1977,** - 44.5°C

Source: Environment Canada; Edmonton Public Library.

PASS THE SHOVEL

About 27 percent of Edmonton's annual precipitation falls as snow. The city gets an average 123.5 cm of the white stuff each year, making Edmonton the 73rd snowiest city in Canada with nowhere near Gander, NL's, annual 443 cm of snowfall.

Edmontonians can expect an average of 54 days of snow a year, far fewer than Val-d'Or, Quebec's 103.5 snow days (the greatest in Canada) but considerably more than the mere 9.7 days of snow that Victoria, BC gets each year (the least in Canada).

In the spring, Edmonton gets on average 33.69 cm of snow and in the fall, an average 27.19 cm. Edmonton has snow on the ground for 130.64 days a year, 60 days fewer than Yellowknife, the Canadian city with the longest snow cover and about 126 days more than Duncan, BC, the Canadian city that enjoys the shortest snow cover.

Edmonton suffers from three days of blowing snow a year and can expect heavy snow (of 25 cm or more) on just .16 days each year.

Source: Environment Canada.

Did you know...

that of the prairie provincial capitals, Edmonton receives the most snow?

that the average snowflake falls at a speed of 5 km/hr?

SNOW REMOVAL COSTS

In 2006, Edmonton's budget for winter road maintenance was $34.4 million.

PLOUGH PROBLEMS

The winter of 2006 was an easy one with just 35 cm of snowfall. However, when 30 cm blanketed the city in a late snowfall on March 17-18, traffic was snarled. The reason? Given the snow-free season, many plough operators had been lured north to the oil fields where their services were needed. Only 55 of the city's 135 ploughs were available to clear streets after this St. Paddy's day storm.

Black Friday

Tornadoes have been known to appear in skies over Edmonton. But no one was prepared for the devastation wrought by a mammoth twister that touched down on "Black Friday."

Friday, July 31, 1987 was a warm day, marked by severe thunderstorms. Shortly after 3 p.m., a twister was spied in nearby Leduc, prompting the issuance of a tornado warning. The warning proved to be warranted as moderate F-2 and F-3 storms spawned in the city's southeast end. The worst was yet to come.

At 3:25 p.m. a deadly storm, a strong F-4 category, ploughed through the northeast end of the city. With a deafening roar, winds, rain and hail the size of tennis balls devastated sections of Edmonton in a rampage that lasted nearly an hour. It cut a swath that was 37 km in length, ranging from 10 m to 1000 m in width.

The destruction was staggering. Twenty seven people were dead, all from the east end of the city. Another 600 were injured, 53 needing hospitalization. Hundreds of homes were destroyed and 1,700 people were left homeless. Property damaged topped a staggering $300 million. Black Friday was the worst natural disaster in Alberta's history and the second most calamitous in Canada's history.

They Said It

> "Edmonton is also, it must be said, about the coldest city in Christendom. No one knows the meaning of the word cold who has not waited for a bus on a street corner near the University of Alberta campus on a windy and overcast evening in February."
> – **Mechtild Hoppenrath and Charles Oberdorf,**
> **writers, First Class Canada, 1987.**

DREAMING OF A WHITE CHRISTMAS

Edmonton has an 88 percent chance of having a white Christmas but it has only a 20 percent chance of a "perfect Christmas," one with snow in the air and at least 2 cm on the ground.

December 25, 1997, was an historic Christmas day. With temperatures nearing 7°C, it was Edmonton's first "brown" Christmas in 100 years. It also stands in contrast to the Christmas of 1961 when the city recorded its highest Christmas day snowfall, 4.1 cm. The Christmas of 1987 was the mildest ever, at 9.3°C.

Take 5 THE FIVE COLDEST MONTHLY WIND CHILL RECORDS
FROM NOVEMBER TO MARCH

1. **November 26, 1985**, -50.2°C
2. **December 15, 1964**, -55.5°C
3. **January 26, 1972**, - 61.1°C
4. **February 2, 1989**, -50.7°C
5. **March 4, 1955**, -44°C

Source: Environment Canada.

BONE CHILLING WINDS

Edmontonians have to endure about 67.8 days of the year when wind chills fall below -20°C. Stalwart Edmontonians also withstand nearly 30 days of wind chills below -30°C and 8.1 days of temperatures that feel colder than -40°C.

THE GREAT BLIZZARD OF '89

In 1989, a deceptive January thaw toward the end of the month turned to deadly cold on the 30th as temperatures plunged from 2°C to -25°C. Rain that was falling that morning became a record-breaking 35 cm snowfall by noon. Snow continued to fall and temperatures remained in the -30°C range for days. Seven deaths were directly attributed to the blizzard.

New Year's Destruction

New Year's Day of 1973 dawned with balmy warm weather. People busily prepared for their New Year's Day dinners and get-togethers, completely unaware of what that night would hold in store for them.

Weather forecasters, however, were looking at early morning weather maps with alarm. They realized that all the ingredients for an explosive storm were in place. Although sunny skies and melting snow prevailed, the first blizzard warning hit the wires near nine a.m. Most people paid no attention until the storm was much closer.

Severe blizzard conditions first struck Fort St. John with a vengeance during the noon hour and then roared through Edmonton shortly after midnight. Shortly after the storm struck, a 707 aircraft crashed on approach to the Edmonton International Airport and lost every one of its crew members. Highways were blocked, and the loss of power and communications in some rural areas made survival difficult. It was weeks before all roads had been cleared and all power had been restored.

LIGHTNING

Edmonton gets 85 lightning flashes per 100 km. Comparatively, Canada's most lightning prone city, Windsor, gets 251 flashes per 100 km.

Source: Environment Canada.

MODERATE WINDS

Thanks to tornadoes and Alberta clippers, Edmonton has earned a reputation as a windy place. This designation is, however, misplaced. Year round, the city's average wind speed is 12.12 km/h, making Edmonton only the 61st windiest city in Canada. In comparison, St. John's, Canada's windiest city, records winds blowing at an average 23.3 km/h. Still, Edmonton is considerably windier than Kelowna, Canada's least windy city where wind speeds average just 5.38 km/h.

The highest wind gust recorded in the city was 146 km/h, measured on October 1, 1965. Such breezy weather is not that common, however. Over the past 50 years wind gusts have only surpassed 100 km/h on 21 occasions.

Did you know...

that in the aftermath of Black Friday, the Insurance Bureau of Canada paid out 50,000 successful claims for hail damage to cars?

Did you know...

that northern lights occur as a result of solar particles colliding with the gases in the earth's atmosphere?

THE WILDEST WINDS

Despite the notoriety of Black Friday, tornadoes are not common in Edmonton. In fact, only 18 have been recorded in the last 100 years and most caused very little damage.

ALL HAIL TO EDMONTON

Edmonton receives an average 56 days of hail a year.

EXTREME WEATHER CONTEST: EDMONTON V. CALGARY

Thunderstorms (number per year per 1000 km^2)
Edmonton: 2.3   Calgary: 1.6

Hail Events (Walnut size or larger, per year, per 1000 km^2)
Edmonton: 0.8   Calgary: 0.7

Heavy Rain Events (30 mm or more /hour)
Edmonton: 0.5   Calgary: 0.4

Tornado Sightings (per decade per 1000 km^2)
Edmonton: 0.8   Calgary: 0.1

Source: University of Alberta.

Weblinks

The 1987 Edmonton Tornado Atlas

www.iassistdata.org/tornado/t87.html#Contents

Robert B. Charlton, Bradley M. Kachman and Lubomir Wojtiw of the University of Alberta compiled this report which is an extensive look at Black Friday. Surveys on the tornado's destruction along with rain, thunderstorm and hail statistics are included in this thorough Atlas.

Weather Winners

www.on.ec.gc.ca/weather/winners/intro-e.html

The weather is a topic that most conversations get around to eventually. If you want to know more about Edmonton's weather claim-to-fames, check out this site maintained by Environment Canada.

Crime and Punishment

CRIME LINE

1874: North West Mounted Police set up their first Edmonton-area detachment under the command of Inspector Griesbach, father of Major General Griesbach.

1885: Families from St. Albert and surrounding areas rush into Fort Edmonton after (false) rumours that Fort Saskatchewan has come under siege by Natives urged on by Louis Riel. The fort, which never comes under attack, is filled with provisions.

1892: The town council passes Bylaw 15, giving itself the authority to appoint a special constable for a period of 30 days. The time provision creates a great deal of uncertainty about job security and as a result, few people apply for the job.

1893: Edmonton hires its first constable, John Flynn, newly arrived from Ireland. Flynn's term is short lived and within two months he resigns to seek adventure in the Rockies.

1900: A.E. Pattison is appointed Edmonton's first full-time Chief of Police and a request is made to appoint Emma Robinson as female constable later that year. Council refuses to offer Robinson full-time employment, but she works part-time for the Edmonton City Police and the RCMP until her 1931 retirement.

1907: Garry Barrett is hanged in Edmonton.

1909: Alex Decoteau, a Cree from the Red Pheasant Reserve near North Battleford, Saskatchewan, joins the Edmonton Police, the first Native Canadian to be hired full-time by a municipal police department.

1914: Police Chief A.C. Lancey is accused of running a protection racket against the city's prostitutes. An investigation finds no criminal wrongdoing but charges Chief Lancey with grave misconduct. Lancey leaves the force in disgrace.

1919: Just four months after returning from active service in WWI, Constable William Nixon is shot while responding to reports of gunfire in downtown Edmonton. His killer, John Gundard Larson, is tracked down and arrested.

1952: When the oil discoveries of the 1940s lead to a population boom in Edmonton, the city scrambles to find recruits to staff a larger police force. Fifty experienced officers from Scotland and Ireland are hired and forced to work the beat without uniforms and armed only with whistles and flashlights. Some Edmontonians mistake the unfamiliar new cops for burglars and pounce on them in the street.

1960: Robert Raymond Cook, the last man to be executed in Alberta, is hanged in Edmonton.

1962: Edmonton pro golfer, Frank Willey, goes missing. William Huculak and Raymond Daniel Workman are convicted of murdering Willey, although his body is never recovered.

The Murder of Punky Gustavson

Six-year-old Corinne "Punky" Gustavson was only out of her parents' sight for a minute when she was abducted in September 1992. The city held its breath as volunteers searched for the young girl. Then came the news everyone dreaded. On September 6, a trucker discovered the little girl's body lying in the mud of an east-end parking lot. She had been sexually assaulted and then smothered.

For Edmonton Police, this awful discovery was the start of a decade of work. Lacking adult witnesses, police had, at best, a vague description of the killer. Their only clues were a hair sample discovered on the body and footprints left at the scene of the abduction.

At the time, the hair could not yield a DNA "fingerprint," but investigators hoped that technological advancements would render it useful in the near future. The footprints were intriguing. As they were cleat marks, they suggested that the killer was a baseball player. Indeed, there had been a baseball tournament held in nearby Sherwood Park when Punky went missing. Every player in the tournament was investigated, but no solid suspects emerged.

Meanwhile, detectives slogged through over 5,000 tips, many of them bogus. Punky's neighbourhood was home to several convicted sex offenders, but all had alibis. All were asked to submit a DNA test. All complied and were removed as suspects. By 1994, the trail was cold.

It was not until 2000 that a break came in the case. That year, federal law established a national DNA databank of serious and serial sex offenders and new DNA technology for the first time allowed police to identify the DNA of the suspect whose hair had been found at the scene. DNA samples were poured over once more. The rejuvenated investigation led to Clifford Sleigh, who was already serving time for sexual assault. In March 2003, Sleigh confessed to killing Punky Gustavson. He was sentenced to life in prison.

1971: Robert Neville is killed in his downtown travel agency office. His former business partner and Queen's University professor Keith Latta is convicted of the crime.

1988: A sextrade worker is found murdered, abandoned in a field. She is the first victim in an as yet ongoing spate of murders of women in western Canada.

1990: Officer Ezio Faraone is killed while pursuing two suspects in a bank robbery.

1994: Tim Orydzuk and James Deiter are found dead in a Sherwood Park industrial plant. Initial reports say they died of electrocution, but it is later determined that the men were shot in the head. Jason Dix, a friend and coworker of the victims, is arrested.

1995: In a gruesome crime, Donald Smart kills Jo-Anne Dickson, assaults her dead body, dismembers her remains, places them in a suitcase, and tosses it in the North Saskatchewan River.

1996: Prosecutors realize they cannot convict Jason Dix of murder and drop charges against him.

2002: Jason Dix wins a malicious prosecution trial against the RCMP and Crown Prosecutor and is awarded $715,000 in damages.

2003: Alberta RCMP "K" Division launches Project Kare, a multi-jurisdictional, multiple force effort to crack several unsolved homicides involving women who worked in the sex trade in Edmonton.

2004: Edmonton banker Nick Lysyk is sentenced to seven years behind bars for stealing $16.5 million through phony loans from an Edmonton branch of the Bank of Montreal where he worked.

2005: Edmonton earns the dubious distinction as "Canada's Murder Capital," recording 44 homicides in the calendar year, ten more than in 2004.

2006: In October, Michael Ritter, former Chief Parliamentary Counsel to the Alberta Legislature, pleads guilty to fraud and stealing $10.5 million from a U.S. energy trader.

CRIME BY THE NUMBERS

Crime is a fact of life in any Canadian city and Edmonton is no exception. The rate of crime in Edmonton is 126 per 1,000 population, compared to a national rate of 77.6 crimes per 1,000.

Here's how crime rates have fared this century.

Offense	2001	2005	Change (%)
Total violent crimes	7,678	6,718	-13
Assault	5,538	4,756	-16
Sexual assault	562	393	-43
Homicide	30	44	+50
Total property crimes	41,061	54,520	+33
Break and enter	7,166	8,713	+21
Vehicle theft	6,586	9,561	+45
All other theft	20,746	29,441	+42
Possess stolen goods	2,146	2,379	+11
Fraud	4,417	4,426	Nil

CRIME STATS

Edmonton has the 5th highest crime rate of all Canadian cities with more than 100,000 people and takes 3rd place among the nine Canadian cities with populations over 500,000. Edmonton's crime rate fell by two percent in 2005.

When it comes to other crimes, however, Edmonton fares much better in a national comparison. In Edmonton you're less likely to have your home broken into than if you were in Vancouver, Saskatoon, Regina, or even St. John's.

OTHER CRIME FIGURES FOR 2005

- 1,492 drug violations
- 36,902 total Criminal Code charges
- 31,541 adult charges
- 5,151 youth charges

Source: Edmonton Police Service; City of Edmonton; CBC.

JAIL BIRDS

Edmonton is home to the Edmonton Institution, a federal maximum-security institution. It has a total capacity of 264 prisoners, plus a medium- and minimum-security area for up to 45 female offenders. Fort Saskatchewan Correctional Centre is just a short drive away.

Fifty-five percent of prisoners in Alberta are serving an actual sentence, while 45 percent are held under temporary detention.

REMAND

Edmonton is home to the provincial Edmonton Remand Centre, an adult center for remand. Although it houses 700 prisoners, it was only designed for 388. In fact, the Centre is so overcrowded that judges often award two days against a sentence for every day served in Remand. On New Year's Eve 2006, the population of the already-crowded facility grew by one when a 25-year old inmate gave birth to a baby, one of Edmonton's New Year's babies.

Source: The Edmonton Journal; Alberta Solicitor General; Correctional Services Canada.

A Hitchcockian Crime:
The Latta-Neville Murder case

On Sunday, June 13, 1971, Bob Neville, a school trustee and travel agency owner, was found murdered in his downtown office. Puzzled Edmonton police predicted a long investigation. This was, however, not to be the case. Just six days later, a Kingston, Ontario law professor, Keith Latta — a former partner in Neville's travel agency — was charged with Neville's murder.

The first clue in the case came in the form of a revolver discovered in Mayfair (Hawrelak) Park that matched the murder weapon. Then the murder scene yielded a hand-drawn map and a locker key. The map, written in Italian, led police to the Greyhound station and a locker there contained an Italian/English dictionary, an Italia Airlines map and bullet cartridges that matched the gun from the park, all wrapped in a *Calgary Herald* newspaper. Initially police deduced that an Italian hit man had flown to Calgary, taken a bus to Edmonton, killed Neville in his office, and tossed his murder weapon in Mayfair Park.

Latta, meanwhile, informed police that he had traveled to Edmonton the day of the murder because Neville had said he was in trouble with some shady characters. On the Sunday of the crime, Latta claimed he waited at a hotel for a call from Neville, but when the call never came, he returned to Ontario. The police knew there was more to the story. The newspaper found at the bus station was emblazoned with Latta's fingerprints and left hand palm print.

Police also deduced a motive. While Latta and Neville had been partners, they had taken out life insurance policies — worth $37,500 — on each other's lives. In the event of a violent death, the policy was to double. The policies remained in place even after Latta left the business.

The evidence and motive were enough for police; Latta was arrested and charged with murder and a jury later found him guilty. The "Italian hit man" theory was discredited. As the prosecutor noted of that theory, "Surely no paid killer leaves that many calling cards around so carelessly." And so, Keith Latta was sentenced to life in prison for killing Bob Neville.

Edmonton's Stolen Sisters

A black cloud hangs over the city of Edmonton. For three decades, Edmonton women have disappeared or have been found dead. Tragically, because many of these women are transients, living risky lives connected to the drug and sex trades, few people batted an eye. It was only after William Pickton's arrest for the multiple slayings of women sextrade workers from Vancouver's lower east side that alarm bells sounded in Edmonton.

In 2002, the RCMP and Edmonton City Police initiated a review of all unsolved missing person cases in Alberta, Saskatchewan, Manitoba and the Territories. The results were shocking. They showed 125 unsolved missing persons and homicide cases involving people linked to so-called "risky" lifestyles. Of these, 25 were linked specifically to the Greater Edmonton Area, dating back to 1975. The victims in these cases are almost exclusively women (only four males are part of the Alberta investigation), and First Nations women are disproportionately represented. Phase Two of the project, the creation of an information database related to the cases, is still underway. It is anticipated that this database will yield common threads in the cases, helping to identify suspects.

Project Kare, the name given to the third investigational phase of the missing persons project, began in October 2003, and involves the RCMP, Criminal Intelligence Service of Alberta, the Edmonton Police Service and the Blood Tribe Police Service. Crown prosecutor Clifton Purvis has been assigned to the project full-time, tasked with preparing a case (or cases) in advance of arrests. The Alberta Government has offered $100,000 for any tips leading to the arrest and conviction of a suspect in the Project Kare file.

Project Kare has not been without is critics and there is reason for disappointment about its work. Since it's launch in 2003, ten more women have been murdered in the Edmonton vicinity.

ARMAMENT AMNESTY

In November 2006, Police Chief Mike Boyd authorized a "gun amnesty" to get unused weapons off the street. Here's what was floating around Edmonton:

- 72 handguns
- 405 long guns
- 223 shot guns
- 23 air guns
- 45 pellet guns
- 6 starter pistols
- 1 flare gun

Source: Alberta Justice.

EDMONTON'S POLICE HELICOPTER BY THE NUMBERS (2005)

- Operating costs per year: $585,000
- Salaries for four flying constables: $376,000
- Number of "criminal flight cases" managed (no pun intended): 55
- Calls responded to: 2784
- Number of "pro-active patrols" of "high-risk areas": 643
- Number of vehicle stops monitored: 220
- Average time to respond to a call, in seconds: 90
- Number of crimes prevented: unknown

Source: Edmonton Police Commission.

IT'LL COST YA

Failure to keep your metre filled in Edmonton will cost you $35. Park in an alley or on a sidewalk or obstruct traffic and you're on the hook for $40-$50 dollars. And if your parallel parking skills are not up to snuff that'll cost you $30. Here are some other traffic no-nos and their penalties:

- Park large vehicle in residential area: $110.00
- Prohibited parking - emergency exit door: $150.00
- Prohibited parking - entrance to firehall/hospital: $150.00
- Prohibited parking - emergency access route: $150.00

- Park in disabled parking zone: $150.00
- Park obstructing emergency vehicles: $150.00
- Abandon vehicle on highway: $200.00
- Abandon vehicle on public/private property: $200.00

BITING INTO CRIME

Since its inception in 1983, the Edmonton and Northern Alberta chapter of Crime Stoppers has taken a huge bite out of crime.

- Arrests: 6,461
- Value of recovered stolen property: $14,059,977
- Value of drugs seized: $46,855,507
- Criminal cases cleared: 12,853
- Value of awards approved: $1,195,864

Source: Crimestoppers.

TRAFFIC CRIME AND ACCIDENTS BY THE NUMBERS (2005)

- 31,775 collisions
- 26 fatal collisions
- 6,148 non-fatal injuries
- 171,545 speeding tickets
- 12,571 red lights ignored
- 5,528 hit and run incidents
- 1,972 charges for driving with a suspended license
- 1,427 cases of impaired driving
- 219 cases of dangerous driving
- 180 cases of dangerous driving while trying to evade the police

Source: Edmonton Police Service.

STOLEN CARS

In all, 484 cars per 100,000 people are stolen in Edmonton each year, the 7th most of major cities in Canada.

Take 5 POLICE CHIEF MIKE BOYD'S TOP FIVE WAYS TO ACHIEVE A SAFER COMMUNITY

Chief Boyd has been guiding the Edmonton Police Service since January 1, 2006, after spending 35 years with the Toronto Police Service. Chief Boyd is committed to reducing victimization through intelligence-led policing, combating organized crime and improved problem-solving techniques. He believes a safer community can be achieved by developing strong working relationships with the 'Big 5' — the community (both business and residential), social and government agencies, the media, political leaders at all levels and the police.

1. **Work together to solve problems.** It is only through continuous collaboration between citizens, businesses, social and government agencies, political leaders, police and the media that we can identify issues of crime and disorder and develop viable and sustainable solutions.

2. **Keep a cool head in the face of conflict.** The old saying it's better to walk away from a fight stills hold true today.

3. **Help our young people make healthy and positive choices.** Everyone who interacts with children or teenagers, including parents, caregivers, educators, police and other peers, can provide these young people with the right tools and support to make good decisions.

4. **Hold all people accountable for their actions**. Those who make choices to victimize or hurt others must know there are consequences for such actions and will be held responsible.

5. **Stand up for the most basic human values of dignity,** respect and acceptance, for self and others. If we're going to build a safer community for everyone, we must each find our own way to speak out against violence and crime, and then get back to the basics of how we treat one another.

Bio BERNIE EBBERS

It seems unlikely that one of the world's all-time biggest white-collar criminals would hail from Edmonton. After all, to achieve such notoriety, one has to first become one of the world's largest businessmen. Bernard Ebbers has, however, made a career out of exceeding expectations.

Born in Edmonton in August 1941, Ebbers was a pretty average kid. He was an average basketball player who chased girls, and while clever, did not excel at school. When he dropped out of a Physical Education degree started at the University of Alberta, he tried his hand at a Christian College in the United States. He failed again and then returned to Edmonton to work as a milkman and a bouncer. His high school basketball coach pulled some strings and got him into the Baptist Mississippi College where he finished his degree.

Within a few years of graduation, Ebbers had moved from working as a warehouse manager to owning a hotel chain, having convinced friends to lend him money to start that venture. In 1983, he turned his attention to the phone business.

In a series of business takeovers in the 1990s, Ebbers transformed his one-time penny stock company LDDS into Worldcom, the largest fibre-optics communications line owner in North America just as the Internet boomed.

Ebbers' roaring Internet success story — Worldcom was valued at $180 billion in 1999 — would, however, be short lived. The dotcom bubble burst in 2000 and Worldcom started fudging its books.

When no clients rented bandwidth on a massive fibre-optics network that Worldcom leased from other owners, Ebbers and other execs used creative accounting and counted the lease expense of the network as a company asset. In short, revenues were inflated and shady accounting continued when Ebbers took a loan from Worldcom to pay off personal debts.

In March 2002, Ebbers resigned in the middle of an accounting investigation, just months before Worldcom declared bankruptcy. In March 2005, a U.S. Federal Court convicted Ebbers of an $11 billion fraud that drove Worldcom into bankruptcy, destroyed 20,000 jobs, and cost investors $180 billion.

DRUG OFFENSES (2005)

- Total drug offenses:1,492
- Cocaine: 589
- Cannabis: 471
- Methamphetamine: 299
- Number involving heroin: 0
- Other: 199

Source: City of Edmonton.

PROSTITUTION

The incidence of prostitution has fallen markedly in Edmonton since 2001 when there were 884 such offenses. In 2005, there were 477.

PROJECT KARE: A PROGRESS REPORT

Despite the resources behind Project Kare, critics maintain that law enforcement continued to neglect the problem of missing and murdered women. Reporters have called on police to release victims' names and in 2004 an Amnesty International report alleged that western Canadian police forces' failure to address the disproportionately high victimization rate of First Nations' women constitutes a violation of international human rights conventions.

Project Kare has, however, had some success. For example, in May 2006, Thomas George Svekla was arrested in the murder case of 36 year-old Theresa Innes, an inner-city sextrade worker. Following his arrest, an *Edmonton Sun* columnist revealed that Svekla claimed to be a "person of interest" in the death of Rachelle Quinney, a teenaged prostitute. Svekla told the columnist that he had found Quinney's body just outside of Edmonton in 2004.

The arrest of Svekla, however, sent up a red flag for the media. Why had police failed to issue a missing person's bulletin when Innes disappeared? Corporal Wayne Oakes, a spokesman for RCMP "K" division, says that it was not up to the RCMP to issue a bulletin as Innes had been reported missing to Edmonton Police, and a missing persons report can endanger women hiding from an abuser. Police also counter media demands for a complete list of the victims, alleging that the media scrutiny that would surround the releasing of such a list would "re-victimize" families of murdered and disappeared.

Corporal Oakes insists that Kare has, in fact, produced satisfactory results, noting that the cases are extraordinarily difficult ones of the sort that usually go on for decades. He adds that "investigators live, work and breathe to solve these cases. It doesn't matter who the person is; in every circumstance the person is a victim. That's what their focus is on."

JUSTICE DENIED: THE JASON DIX CASE, PART I

It was October 1, 1994, and Stephanie Orydzuk was furious at her husband, Tim, for not picking up their daughter at noon as promised. The irate wife traveled to the industrial warehouse in Sherwood Park where Tim worked. There she made a horrifying discovery of the lifeless bodies of her husband and his co-worker, James Deiter.

RCMP Constable Donald Drissell answered the 911 call. At the scene he hastily concluded that both men had been electrocuted. It was only after an autopsy that the shocking truth of their deaths emerged. The victims had each been shot three times in the head.

The embarrassed RCMP officials now faced a huge obstacle. Having proclaimed the site a workplace accident, crime scene evi-

Did you know...

that in 1913 Edmonton appointed the first full-time "policewoman" in Canada, Annie M. Jackson? Her duties included the enforcement of morals and manners amongst young girls in Edmonton. The appointment was reported in the London Daily Mirror on Friday August 8, 1913, which noted that the female officer's work resulted in an immediate decrease in "hoydenish behaviour" amongst young women in Edmonton.

dence had been compromised and the investigation had no choice but to turn to people close to the victims for answers. Before long, police closed in on one man, Jason Dix, and they went to extraordinary lengths to convict him.

The RCMP theory was centred on a motive of jealousy. Investigators claimed that Dix was either worried that Deiter would reveal an affair that he had been having with a coworker, or was angry that Deiter himself had a love interest in the woman. According to the theory, Tim Orydzuk had simply been in the wrong place at the wrong time. There were, however, some significant problems with this theory. The RCMP had no evidence and Jason Dix had an airtight alibi.

A lack of evidence didn't stop the Mounties. To prove that Dix was capable of murder, undercover RCMP officers posed as gangsters, drawing Dix into a make-believe world of crime. In long conversations with the phony crime lords, Dix offered suggestions on how to "whack" a target. At no point, however, was Dix cajoled into admitting he had committed the murder.

Eventually, undercover cops staged a "shoot-out" complete with exploding blood packs. An RCMP officer posing as "Mr. Big" told Dix that if he was ever fingered for the Orydzuk-Deiter murders it could hurt the "organization." The "gangsters" promised to arrange an alibi for him. Dix refused to budge.

Still, the Mounties pursued Dix. They interviewed his wife, his four-year-old son and his mistress. They bugged his phone, his car and his bedroom, all to no avail. Finally the Mounties discovered a cache of weapons at a cabin visited by Dix shortly after the murder. On July 10, 1996, the RCMP arrested Jason Dix.

(MIS)TRIAL OF THE CENTURY: THE JASON DIX CASE, PART II

After his arrest for the murders of Tim Orydzuk and James Deiter, Jason Dix faced 11 hours of interrogation and was placed in a holding cell with an undercover officer. Dix confessed nothing. Not to be deterred, the RCMP paid jailhouse informants to try and get a confession; still nothing. The incredible pressure wore on Dix and he tried to commit suicide.

Dix was denied bail when police received a letter from an informant stating that a witness might be "eliminated" before the trial. This letter in hand, the Crown Prosecutor, Arnold Piragoff, convinced the judge to keep Dix in custody until the trial.

After 22 months behind bars, Dix got his day in court. Within three weeks the case ground to a standstill, the biggest hurdle being the lack of evidence. The crux of the Crown's case was informant testimony, but this was disallowed by the judge who deemed the informants to be "reprehensible" and unreliable.

The final blow to the Crown's case came when Dix's defense revealed that the letter used to withhold bail from Dix was not written by an informant, but was an RCMP forgery. Even worse, the Crown prosecutor knew it was a fake. With this stunning revelation, the case against Jason Dix dissolved. Charges were dropped and by 1998 Jason Dix was a free man.

In the end it was the RCMP and Piragoff who would be convicted. A civil suit concluded in 2002 awarded Dix $715,000 in damages for "malicious prosecution" by Piragoff and six officers. The murders of Orydzuk and Deiter remain unsolved.

Weblinks

Hot Cars of the Day

www.police.edmonton.ab.ca/Pages/Media/hotcars.asp

Check out this website to find out what vehicles have recently been stolen in Edmonton.

Great Alberta Law Cases

www.albertasource.ca/lawcases/audio2.htm

A project of the Alberta Online Encyclopedia, this site offers print and audio resources surrounding important Edmonton court cases.

Culture

Edmonton is home to people of an array of backgrounds and ethnicities, all of whom celebrate their cultures in their hometown. Now widely known as "Festival City," Edmonton boasts year round events that celebrate this colourful combination of cultural traditions.

THE CAPITAL OF CULTURE

In 2005, the Edmonton Arts Council spread more than $2.76 million worth of support around the city in the form of grants, while Edmontonians paid $82.5 million to enjoy cultural events. That year, the arts contributed $123.7 million to the city's GDP and 3.9 million Edmontonians took in arts and culture events. In 2007, the Government of Canada designated Edmonton "Canada's Cultural Capital." This award resulted in about $2 million in funding for artistic and cultural projects for the year, $667,000 of which came from the city.

Source: City of Edmonton; Edmonton Arts.

ARTISTS

- Number of artists in Canada: 130,700 (0.8 percent of the workforce)
- Number in Edmonton: 3,095 (0.8 percent of the workforce)
- Edmonton artists' average earnings: $20,000
- Gap between artists' earnings and overall workforce average: 35 percent

Take 5 TOP FIVE MOST-ATTENDED FESTIVALS IN EDMONTON

1. **Edmonton Klondike Days Festival** (546,500)
2. **Edmonton Fringe Festival** (460,000)
3. **The Works: A Visual Arts Celebration** (215,000)
4. **International Street Performers Festival** (200,000)
5. **Heritage Festival** (179,000)

Source: AlbertaFirst.

EDMONTON HAS:

- 190 actors
- 425 artisans and craftspersons
- 75 conductors, composers and arrangers
- 230 dancers
- 885 musicians and singers
- 155 other performers
- 360 painters, sculptors and other visual artists
- 355 producers, directors, choreographers and related artists
- 430 writers

Source: Canadian Council for the Arts.

GALLERIES AND MUSEUMS

Edmonton is home to 25 museums and 60 art galleries.

Did you know...

that the Edmonton area represented by the postal code 'T6G' — surrounding the University of Alberta campus — boasts the highest concentration of artists in Alberta? About two percent of the labour force there consists of artists.

Take 5 TOP FIVE ITEMS ON WHICH EDMONTONIANS SPENT THEIR CULTURAL DOLLARS
(PERCENT)

1. **Home Entertainment** (49)
2. **Reading Materials** (19)
3. **Art Works and Events** (12)
4. **Photographic Equipment and Services** (10)
5. **Movie Theatre Admissions** (6)

Source: Canada Council for the Arts..

RECOGNITION FOR THE ARTS

In 2006, the Canada Council of the Arts awarded $7 million in grants to artists and cultural organizations in Alberta. In addition, $400,000 was given to 747 authors through the Public Lending Right Program that year, bringing the total funding to the province to $7.4 million.

Of the total, just over $2.9 million — or 41 percent — went to support artists of all disciplines in the city, including arts, music, media arts, theatre, visual arts, writing and publishing.

Source: Canadian Council for the Arts.

CULTURAL SPENDING

Edmontonians were among the highest cultural spenders in Canada. Indeed, the city ranked 5th among Canadian cities. In 2005, Edmontonians spent a total of $930 million on culture goods and services — that's $952 each.

Edmontonians come 4th when it comes to buying art and paying to attend cultural events. On average, they spent $116 on these things in 2005, considerably more than the Canadian average of $88, and just slightly less than Calgary ($139), Ottawa-Gatineau ($121) and St. John's ($117).

Source: Hill Strategies Research Inc.

ORCHESTRATING MUSIC

Since 1952, the Edmonton Symphony Orchestra (ESO) has been a bastion of high culture in Edmonton. The orchestra has attracted some big names in classical music but its most famous recording session was probably with '70s rock band Procol Harum. The resultant multi-platinum album — "Live with the Edmonton Symphony Orchestra" was released in 1972. Much acclaimed, it spawned the hit single "Conquistador" and inspired other collaborations between rock bands and orchestras.

Indeed, the ESO itself has succeeded with other similar ventures including its 1989 "Symphony Sessions with Tom Cochrane and Red Rider," and the 2003 "Semi-Conducted" with the group the Arrogant Worms.

THE AL-RASHID MOSQUE

A piece of Edmonton's religious history nearly became a parking lot in 2000. The Al-Rashid Mosque, North America's first (built in 1938), was saved by a group of Muslim women who successfully had it declared a Heritage Site and relocated it to Fort Edmonton Park.

Al-Rashid's history is an extraordinary one. The renowned Indian Islamic scholar, Abdullah Yusuf Ali, translator of one of the most respected English editions of Koran, was present at the founding of the mosque and laid the cornerstone of the historic building. The Mosque served the Muslim community for many years until larger mosques began to take its place, and the building fell into disrepair.

FESTIVAL CITY

Edmonton is home to more than 30 festivals each year. Featuring food, performance arts, film, street performers and music of all genres,

Did you know...

that in 1908 Edmonton was home to the first music festival in Canada?

Edmonton makes a festival of all of 'em. Alberta Community Development estimates that 52 percent of Edmontonians attend festivals.

Bio   BANKIN' ON TOMMY BANKS

Born in Calgary in 1936, Tommy Banks moved to Edmonton with his family in 1949, and has stayed ever since. Jazz musician, symphony conductor, television host, founding Chairman of the Alberta Foundation for the Performing Arts, Officer of the Order of Canada and Senator all describe Tommy Banks.

His musical talent has been at the centre of many major events in Canada. In 1978, he directed the music for the Edmonton Commonwealth Games, and did the same for Vancouver's Expo '86 and Calgary's 1988 Winter Olympic Games. In 1983, Banks went international, becoming the first musician to lead a jazz quintet on tour through the People's Republic of China.

Banks left his biggest mark in Edmonton being the musical host of the "Tommy Banks Show," a locally produced and nationally broadcast talk show that ran from 1968 to 1974, and then again from 1980 to 1983. His success reflects, in part, the city's dedication to the arts, despite its blue-collar reputation and rabid hockey worship.

In recent years, Banks found a niche in politics. In 2000, Prime Minister Jean Chrétien appointed Liberal Banks to the Senate, a provocative political move at a time when Albertans were agitating for senate reform. In 2006, Banks made headlines when a trip that he and other Liberal Senators made to Dubai was denounced for lavish spending. Unable to get clearance to enter Afghanistan where they intended to study Canada's military contribution and expenditures, the delegates unexpectedly had to pay $311 a night for several nights at a Dubai hotel.

Dubbed "Dubai-gate," the controversy earned the ire of critics who argued that the accommodation costs would have been far cheaper than the price of last minute flights out of the Arab state. Not even political mudslinging, however, can take the shine off one of Edmonton's favourite stars.

Take 5   FIVE MOVIES MADE OR CURRENTLY FILMING IN THE GREATER EDMONTON AREA

1. **"Bury My Heart at Wounded Knee"** (with Anna Paquin and Aidan Quinn), in production for 2008.
2. **"The Assassination of Jesse James"** (with Casey Affleck), in production for 2007.
3. **"Good Luck, Chuck"** (with Jessica Alba), in post-production for 2007.
4. **"Intern Academy"** (with Dave Thomas and Dan Akroyd), 2003.
5. **"Snow Day"** (with Chevy Chase), 2000.

NATIONAL ABORIGINAL AWARENESS DAY

Each June 21, Aboriginal people in Edmonton join all other Canadians in celebrating National Aboriginal Awareness Day. First proclaimed by Governor-General Roméo A. LeBlanc, National Aboriginal Awareness Day was first celebrated in 1996.

THAT'S AN ORDER

In all, 153 Edmontonians have been honoured with the Order of Canada. Two are Companions (the highest award), 49 are Officers and 102 are Members.

EDMONTON'S POET LAUREATE

Edmonton has one of several Poet Laureates in Canada. In June 2005, Alice Major became the city's first Poet Laureate. For two years, the Poet Laureate is expected to act as an Ambassador for the city, publish

Did you know...

that actor Michael J. Fox was born in Edmonton? His military family moved away from the city when he was still a toddler.

Take 5 MARTY CHAN'S TOP FIVE EDMONTON THEATRE ACCOMPLISHMENTS

Marty Chan is an Edmonton playwright, humorist, young adult author and television writer. His hit play, "Mom, Dad, I'm Living with a White Girl," has been produced across Canada and in New York. His latest project is a kids' book titled *The Mystery of the Graffiti Ghoul.*

1. **Die-Nasty.** In 1991, some of Edmonton's funniest actors gathered on the Varscona Theatre stage to start a live, improvised soap opera. The show has been running ever since and has featured high-powered guest stars including Mike Myers (Austin Powers), Joe Flaherty (SCTV) and Nathan Fillion (Serenity).

2. **Edmonton Fringe Festival.** This ten-day alternative theatre festival has been the training ground for playwrights. Stewart Lemoine, Brad Fraser, Darrin Hagen, David Belke and Chris Craddock are a few of this festival's luminaries.

3. **University of Alberta BFA program.** Some of Canada's finest actors have studied at this prestigious drama program. Paul Gross (Due South) and Lorne Cardinal (Corner Gas) are probably the most recognisable of the institution's alumni.

4. **Citadel Theatre.** The largest regional theatre in western Canada, this red brick building has been running a full season on all three of its stages for over 40 years. In the 70s, esteemed British actor John Neville served as the theatre's artistic director for five years. Other notable artistic directors include Robin Phillips and Bob Baker.

5. **Edmonton's theatre reputation.** Great playwrights, actors, designers and directors have worked in this city, but what Edmonton's theatre community will be best known for is its unflagging support of theatre artists. Whether you need a hard-to-find prop or a volunteer for a fundraiser, Edmontonians are quick to help and hard to forget.

three original works each year and present works to the city's citizens at least once at City Council, once at a charity event and at least two official city functions. The Poet Laureate must also record all of his or her work and activities and compile an archives. A new Poet Laureate will be named in June 2007.

MOVIE THEATRES (2006)

- Number of Theatres: 16
- Number of Screens: 117
- Average cost of Admission: $8.30

DIE HARD FANS OF DIE-NASTY

The live improvised soap opera Die-Nasty has been playing every year since 1993 at the Varscona Theatre. Dedicated fans show up every Monday night for the unscripted show. Directed by Dana Andersen, Die-Nasty has a new premise each season — even cast members are in the dark about their characters' names and relations with the other actors until the moment they step on stage.

Nathan Fillion, Ron Pederson and Patti Stiles are just a few of the cast who have gone on to Hollywood success. Alternately, established Hollywood actors — including Joe Flaherty, Mark McKinney and Mike Myers — have trekked to Edmonton to try their hand at the show.

Bio W. P. KINSELLA

Don't let Calgarians claim author William Patrick Kinsella. Although Kinsella's hit novel, Shoeless Joe (later made into Kevin Costner's hit movie, "Field of Dreams"), was penned during Kinsella's stint at the University of Calgary, his true roots reach north.

Kinsella was born in Edmonton on May 25, 1935, and grew up on a farm near the community of Darwell, just west of the city. At age ten, his family moved to Edmonton, a city that has clearly influenced his stories.

Many of his stories are centred in Hobbema, a First Nations reserve south of the city. Kinsella claims that he chose the town at random, but admits that a catalyst for the stories was his imagining what would happen if he brought a young Native woman to his family home in downtown Edmonton.

If Edmontonians live boom and bust lives, Kinsella is a model citizen. He loathes both Hollywood and the CBC for what he claims was insufficient compensation for movie and television productions based on his novels and stories.

Kinsella has his own share of critics — some revile him for appropriating the Aboriginal voice, a charge first leveled by fellow Edmonton scribe Rudy Wiebe. Kinsella later claimed this criticism helped him sell 15,000 more books than he would have ordinarily. Such criticisms didn't hurt his stature much, and in 1993 he was named an Officer of the Order of Canada.

In 1997, W.P. Kinsella suffered a serious head injury when he was hit by a car. The injury sidelined his writing until recently, when he took up a regular column at the Vancouver Province. In his column he taunts left-coast readers with homespun wisdom and conservative opinion.

SCTV

The most famous television show produced in Edmonton was Second City Television, SCTV. The show left Toronto for Edmonton in 1980 in a move that was part of a financial arrangement with new backer Charles Allard, a surgeon, businessman and owner of ITV, Edmonton's independent television station.

Actors/comedians Dave Thomas, John Candy, Andrea Martin, Joe Flaherty, Catherine O'Hara and Eugene Levy were in the original cast

Bio   WAYNE GRETZKY

Okay, so technically the Ontario-born Wayne Gretzky is not an Edmontonian, but no book of all things Edmonton would be complete without him. This hockey great left an indelible mark on his adopted city, pumping its citizens with pride and giving them the hope of possibility — not to mention four Stanley Cup wins. Edmonton left its mark on the Great One too. Gretzky wept openly when he was traded.

You would almost think that Gretzky was born wearing skates. As a youngster he was obsessed with hockey, and could that kid play. By thirteen, he had 1000 goals under his belt and the media was already referring to him as the "great" Gretzky.

A pro at just 17 years old, Gretzky played briefly with the World Hockey Association Indianapolis Racers. Then in 1978, his and Edmonton's fates were sealed when this boy from Brantford was traded to the Edmonton Oilers, sporting the now famous 99.

From 1978 to 1988, Gretzky led the Oilers to a series of NHL Stanley Cup victories, justifying Edmonton's claim as the "City of Champions." He also brought his adopted city much pride as a key player in Team Canada's 1984 and 1987 Canada Cup victories.

and made the move to Edmonton in 1980.

Initially the actors and writers had misgivings about uprooting to go to a (then) perceived small city in western Canada. Clearly, though, the show benefited immeasurably from its move. With no distractions from family or friends, the cast, which now included Rick Moranis, flung themselves into their work, churning out classic SCTV characters and sketches.

SCTV moved back to Toronto in 1982 but didn't last long. It

In Edmonton, Gretzky became a celebrity of epic proportions. In 1988, the whole city celebrated as he married American actress Janet Jones. His promise to remain in Edmonton with his Californian wife gave credence to the idea that Edmonton is a city where people could be famous; it was a place where great people wanted to live and where great things could happen.

Unfortunately, this fairy tale was short-lived. On August 9, 1988, Oilers owner Peter Pocklington announced that Gretzky had been traded to the Los Angeles Kings for $15 million. Pocklington, at the time in financial trouble, was accused of putting his personal interests ahead of those of the team and the city and irate fans burnt him in effigy.

Gretzky's image and legend, however, remained unscathed. When Number 99 first returned to Edmonton as part of the Kings, Edmontonians stood in the stands and gave the Great One a four-minute standing ovation. And, in 1999, the same year the 43-year-old Gretzky retired, Edmonton City Council renamed the old Capilano route past Rexall Place hockey arena Wayne Gretzky Drive.

Bio MARSHALL MCLUHAN

One of Canada's "coolest" thinkers of all time also came from the country's coldest urban climate. Marshall McLuhan, famous for his idea that "the medium is the message" and for coining the term "global village," is an Edmontonian by birth.

Born in Edmonton in 1911, McLuhan was three when his family packed up for Winnipeg in 1914. After earning his Master of Arts in English Literature at the University of Manitoba in 1934, he hit the road.

Over the next ten years he taught at Cambridge and the University of Wisconsin, converted to Catholicism, joined the Jesuit University of St. Louis and married. Not bad for a decade! He returned to Canada in 1944 and eventually settled at the University of Toronto.

McLuhan's 1964 best-seller, *Understanding Media* earned praise for its description of technology as an extension of the human body and mind and its criticism that the west was stuck in 19th century ways of thinking. McLuhan became something of a "guru" of communications and was visited by the likes of Andy Warhol, John Lennon and Yoko Ono. In 1977, Woody Allen had McLuhan appear as himself in the movie "Annie Hall," scolding a professor who called himself a Marshall McLuhan expert.

Hollywood aside, McLuhan's ideas had lost much of their currency by his death in 1980. Academics found him frivolous and arrogant and his books poorly researched. It took the advent of the Internet to revive his celebrity. Suddenly the idea of a "global village" united by technology and acting tribally, made sense. The technology/lifestyle oriented *Wired Magazine* launched in 1993 with the declaration that McLuhan was its' "patron saint."

As the internet becomes the de facto delivery technology for text, still images, audio and video, the eccentric English professor's work will only grow more relevant.

They Said It

"In Edmonton, all we did was work on the show. Not only that, a lot of the writing came out of just hanging with people — we'd go out for dinner — if we were staying at the Four Seasons Hotel we'd go for dinner and sit around the coffee shop. Somebody would say something funny and before you knew it you had a sketch. Edmonton was where we did our best work because there simply wasn't anything else for us to do!"

– Actor Rick Moranis of SCTV

went through a permutation with NBC in 1983 before winding down a year later with a cable version on Cinemax. In its heyday SCTV won rave reviews. It scored 13 Emmy nominations and took home two of the awards.

FAST FOOD
Number of Tim Horton's in Canada: 2,611
In Edmonton: 74
Number of McDonald's in Canada: 1,375
In Edmonton: 62
Number of Subways in Canada: 2,172
In Edmonton: 60

Did you know...

that households in Edmonton spent an average of $317 on reading materials and other printed matter in 2005?

Did you know...

that the Princess Theatre is Edmonton's oldest surviving movie theatre? The first movie shown at the Whyte Avenue landmark was the 1915 "The Eagle's Mate," starring Canadian superstar Mary Pickford.

Take 5 FIVE EDMONTON WRITERS

1. **Todd Babiak**, *Choke Hold* and *The Garneau Block*

2. **Minister Faust**, *From the Notebooks of Dr. Brain* and *Coyote Kings of the Space Age Bachelor Pad*

3. **Thomas Wharton**, *Icefields, Salamander, The Logogryph*

4. **Myrna Kostash**, *The Next Canada: In Search of the Future Generation, Bloodlines: A Journey Into Eastern Europe*

5. **Christine Wiesenthal**, *The Half-Lives of Pat Lowther*

A GAME TO REMEMBER

On February 19, 2005, forty Edmontonians skated their way into hockey history in the longest hockey game ever played. For more than ten grueling days the team played on an outdoor rink in temperatures that fluctuated between -15°C to 12°C. When all was said and done, the team had secured a place in the Guinness Book of World Records. The score? Well it was about 1,700 to 1,600, but it's safe to say that everyone was a winner.

STANLEY CUP WINS FOR THE EDMONTON OILERS

- 1990
- 1988
- 1987
- 1985
- 1984

Did you know...

that there are 70 golf courses within a 90-minute drive from Edmonton?

They Said It

"I skate to where the puck is going to be, not where it's been."
– Wayne Gretzky

Weblinks

Royal Alberta Museum

www.royalalbertamuseum.ca

This web site of the Royal Alberta Museum in Edmonton offers information on this impressive institution, home to some of the country's most impressive cultural and natural history collections.

Festival City

www.festivalcity.ca

If you are interested in Edmonton's many festivals, check this out. It is the Internet's prime source for information on each and every one of Edmonton's 30+ annual festivals.

Culture of Edmonton

www.ualberta.ca/edmonton/culture

If you want to know what's happening in the city, this online listing and description of the city's standard cultural offerings, including music, theatre, dinner theatre, dance, art and more, is for you.

Did you know...

that Edmonton's 16 libraries are home to over 1.5 million library books and other materials available for borrowing?

Economy

Located at the cross roads of some of the world's most productive farm-land and the resource-rich northern frontier, Edmonton serves as the coordinating hub for a vast majority of the economic activities that happen in the North. Supply and service industries support an already frenzied energy extraction sector while expanded value-added process-ing of Alberta's massive oil, gas and oilsands reserves is the economic base of the economy.

Agri-food processing, petro-chemical processing, forestry, the life sciences, and nanotechnology are important players in the Edmonton economy. Processing and manufacturing have also increased in impor-tance as the city has sought to diversify its economy. The city has become one of Canada's leading research and education centres, and in the process developed a dynamic and thriving science and technol-ogy sector.

GMP

- Rank of Calgary and Edmonton in terms of Gross Metropolitan Product (GMP) growth among Canada's 20 major metropolises, according to a report published by the Conference Board of Canada: 1, 2

ALBERTA TAXES

- Alberta is the only province the country with no provincial sales tax.
- Federal GST : 6 percent
- Personal income tax rates: 10 percent of taxable income
- Small business corporate tax rate: 3 percent

Source: Canada Customs and Revenue Agency.

TAX FREEDOM DAY (DATE ON WHICH EARNINGS NO LONGER GO TO TAXES, 2007)

Nationally	June 19
Alberta	June 1
New Brunswick	June 14
Prince Edward Island	June 14
Manitoba	June 16
British Columbia	June 16
Ontario	June 19
Nova Scotia	June 19
Saskatchewan	June 14
Quebec	July 26
Newfoundland and Labrador	July 1

Source: The Fraser Institute.

COST OF LIVING

Edmonton's cost of living is among the lowest at all salary levels, according to a North American survey that compared the total cost of living for employees at three different salary levels. The table shows the family income required in each city to maintain the standard of living associated with three income scenarios.

INCOME LEVEL

CITY	$60,000	$80,000	$100,000
Edmonton	$61,830	$81,142	$99,902
Calgary	$62,818	$82,109	$105,317

Take 5 — EDMONTON'S FIVE BIGGEST PROJECTS
(VALUE)

1. **Oil, Gas and Oilsands** ($20.1 billion)
2. **Institutional** ($2.8 billion)
3. **Infrastructure** ($1.3 billion)
4. **Tourism** ($1.2 billion)
5. **Residential** ($.8 billion)

Source: Edmonton Economic Development Corporation.

Ottawa	$63,168	$84,102	$104,699
Phoenix	$66,523	$88,306	$107,644
Montreal	$68,167	$92,594	$113,884
Vancouver	$69,009	$90,927	$112,647
Minneapolis	$70,961	$93,624	$113,927
Toronto	$74,114	$96,439	$122,627
Seattle	$73,723	$98,441	$118,048
Boston	$84,896	$112,115	$133,384
San Jose	$101,077	$144,029	$164,435

Sources: MMK Consulting and Runzheimer Canada

FAMILY INCOME (MEAN ANNUAL INCOME)

Canada	$58,100
Edmonton	$68,100

Source: Statistics Canada.

IN 2005, EDMONTON HOUSEHOLDS SPENT AN AVERAGE $72,215 A YEAR.

Here's how it broke down:

- Income tax: $15,587
- Shelter: $12,662
- Transportation: $9,813

You Said How Much?

Wage data is hourly and is taken from the latest available data.

Financial managers	$44.78
Lawyers	$45.31
Senior managers, health, education, social services	$42.27
School principals	$41.47
Senior government managers and officials	$39.53
Pharmacists	$35.69
Civil engineers	$34.01
Carpenters	$33.96
Software engineers	$33.04
Physiotherapists	$31.26
Occupational therapists	$31.17
Elementary school teachers	$29.94
Registered nurses	$29.84
Administrators, post secondary education, vocational training	$29.82
Veterinarians	$29.25
Secondary school teachers	$28.84
Fire fighters	$26.56
Heavy equipment mechanics	$25.13
Electricians	$24.71
Social workers	$24.48
University professors	$23.91
Plumbers	$23.84
Oil and gas well diggers and workers	$22.65
Writers	$21.79
Retail managers	$21.09
Pipe fitters	$20.50
Legal secretaries	$19.18
Editors	$19.01
Graphic designers	$18.16
Auto mechanics	$16.46
Medical secretaries	$15.84

MORE SALARIES
- Annual salary of the Mayor of Edmonton $121,820.70
- Annual salary of a city councilor $63,638.06
- 2006/2007 salary of Dwayne Roloson, Edmonton Oilers goaltender $4.5 million

Take 5 TOP FIVE MOST COMMON BUSINESSES IN EDMONTON
(NUMBER, 2005)

1. **Retail trade** (4,866)
2. **Professional, scientific and technical services** (2,087)
3. **Accommodation and food services** (1,961)
4. **Construction** (1,498)
5. **Manufacturing** (1,469)

Source: City of Edmonton.

- Food: $7,575
- Insurance/pension payments: $4,236
- Household operation: $3,390
- Clothing: $2,888
- Monetary gifts/contributions: $1,720
- Health care: $1,932
- Tobacco and alcohol: $1,534
- Education: $1,471
- Personal care: $1,187
- Reading material: $317
- Games of chance: $278
- Recreation: $4,561
- Household furnishings and equipment: $2,040

Source: Statistics Canada.

ON AVERAGE, ALBERTANS OWED $58,400. AMOUNT OWING ON:
- Mortgages: $78,100
- Lines of credit: $14,500
- Vehicle loans: $13,000
- Student loans: $ 9,200
- Credit cards/installments: $3,400
- Other: $11,700

Source: Statistics Canada.

GROWING PAINS

- Percentage of Calgarians who say they believe the current pace of growth for the province of Alberta is not manageable, according to a survey by Leger Marketing: 50
- Percentage of Edmontonians who say they believe the current pace of growth for the province of Alberta is not manageable: 41

O . . . T

- Percentage of Montrealers who work more than 50 hours a week: 7
- Percentage of Vancouverites: 16
- Percentage of Torontonians: 20
- Percentage of Calgarians: 24
- Percentage of Edmontonians: 28

Source: Bank of Montreal.

BY THE HOUR

The story of Edmonton's economy can largely be told by its average wages. Edmonton's average hourly wage is $21.73, slightly higher than Calgary's $20.74. Unionized workers make an average of $23.46, compared to the $20.03 earned by the non-unionized. A government town, the highest paying occupations were in public administration ($29.14/hr), followed by educational services ($28.20/hr). Construction workers recorded the third highest wages ($26.39/hr), edging out professional, technical and scientific occupations ($26.03/hr).

Alberta's minimum wage, at $7.00 an hour, is the second lowest in Canada.

NO PARKING

- Median cost of a monthly parking (unreserved rate) in Edmonton: $140
- Median cost of a monthly parking (unreserved rate) in Calgary as of mid-2006: $375
- Median cost in Toronto: $300

Take 5 SAM SHAW'S TOP FIVE EDMONTON RESTAURANTS
FOR A BUSINESS MEETING

Dr. W.A. (Sam) Shaw is the president and CEO of the Northern Alberta Institute of Technology (NAIT). Shaw is known for forging strategic relationships with businesses including several unprecedented partnerships designed to improve access to high-demand technical education. Although he prefers to do most of his business dining in NAIT's award-winning dining room Ernest's, he has several favorites when he steps off campus.

1. **Characters (www.characters.ca)** Excellent ambiance, great food, discrete private room downstairs and a great location to celebrate a business deal. One of the city's leading chefs, Shonn Oborowsky, is a NAIT grad.

2. **Sorrentino's (www.sorrentinos.com)** Carmelo Rago offers fabulous food that is consistently good in a truly Italian atmosphere with great hospitality. Multiple locations around the city, always willing to accommodate and staff are friendly and outgoing.

3. **Hardware Grill (www.hardwaregrill.com)** Great room downstairs for private meetings, always accommodate business requirements, extraordinary staff and consistently outstanding fare. Larry and Melinda are great supporters of the community and have a standard of excellence that is recognized as a winner.

4. **Moose Factory (www.sawmillrestaurant.com)** Convenient location and diverse lunch buffet. Tom Goodchild cooks up fantastic food for business clientele and caters literally to any business in Edmonton.

5. **Jack's Grill (www.jacksgrill.ca)** Fantastic food, nice atmosphere, great menu and serving staff are very accommodating. Peter Jackson has built a reputation on quality, service and intimate surroundings for every business occasion.

- Median cost in Montreal: $259
- Median cost in Vancouver: $194
- Canadian average: $194.51

Source: Colliers International.

DOWNTOWN OFFICE SPACE (MILLIONS OF SQUARE FEET)

Toronto	59.4
Montreal	50.0
Calgary	32.1
Vancouver	22.6
Edmonton	**14.0**
Ottawa	14.0
Winnipeg	12.9
Victoria	7.8

- Average net asking rents for all classes of space in Edmonton were $16.04 per square foot in 2007.

SELF EMPLOYMENT
- Between 2001 and 2005, the number of people that were self-employed in Edmonton increased by 15%, from 70,000 to 81,000.
- And 37 percent of all self-employed workers in Edmonton are women.

TRANSPORTATION INFRASTRUCTURE

Edmonton has long been an important western transportation hub. In March 2007, Edmonton's Mayor Stephen Mandel joined the mayors of Prince Rupert and Prince George in a memorandum of cooperation in support of the proposed transloading mega-facility planned by CN for Prince Rupert, BC. As part of a "Prince Rupert Corridor," Edmonton will continue its role as a major transport hub in North America.

Bio MAX WARD

A self-made aviation mogul filled with bravado and a touch of madness, you could call Max Ward Edmonton's version of Howard Hughes. Born in Edmonton in 1921, Ward realized when he was in his early thirties that he could parlay Alberta's mining boom and his RCAF piloting experience into a lucrative career, flying men into isolated northern areas.

In 1946, he organized his first northern airline, Polaris Charter Co. Ltd., with a single plane. Four crashes and a bankruptcy later, Ward was learning the dangerous new business trial by fire. He picked himself up and in 1953 set up Wardair Ltd. in Yellowknife, moving heavy equipment into sub arctic Canada.

Ward had six planes by 1962 when he moved his head offices to Edmonton and renamed the company Wardair Canada Ltd. Fighting uphill against Canadian regulators who wanted to protect Air Canada's forerunner, Trans Canada Airlines, Ward nonetheless built a charter holiday carrier with an international reputation for quality service. By 1967, Ward took the company public, and just five years after that was Canada's large international passenger charter operator. By the end of the 1970s, Ward had wrapped up his northern-focused charters to focus exclusively on passenger service.

Ward expanded heavily in the early 1980s and grew his airline into the third largest in Canada, with annual revenues of $491 million and assets totalling $456 million by 1986. Ward didn't stop there. In 1987 and 1988, he purchased 12 Airbuses and 16 McDonnell-Douglas MD-88s with plans for further expansion. The debt, combined with booking issues and competitive frequent flyer programs on competing airlines, crippled the company. In 1989 Canadian Pacific bought out Wardair, temporarily saving the company from bankruptcy. The CP company that swallowed Wardair, Canadian Airlines, folded in 2001.

Air

Greater Edmonton is home to four airports: Edmonton International Airport, Edmonton City Centre Airport, Cooking Lake Airport and Villeneuve Airport

The city's major airport, Edmonton International Airport (EIA), covers nearly 7,000 acres and is Canada's northernmost 24-hour international airport. This central stop for domestic and international passenger and transport flights is fog free 99 percent of the time and in ten years its runways have been closed for just three hours. In 2004, the EIA served 4.1 million passengers, earning it the title of fifth busiest airport in Canada when it comes to passenger service. Aided by runways that accommodate the largest of the world's cargo carriers, the EIA moves more than 38 million tonnes of cargo annaually.

Rail

Edmonton is strategically placed on North America's rail grid and is the largest city on the Canadian National's mainline. The Calgary-Edmonton rail corridor is one of the busiest in North America and there are calls for the creation of a high-speed rail network. Edmonton is also a stop on VIA's The Canadian, the quintessentially Canadian three-day train trek that travels between Toronto and Vancouver. The Canadian passes through Edmonton six times a week.

Highway

Edmonton is strategically located at the intersection of the Yellowhead Highway and Alberta's Queen Elizabeth II, which leads south to Calgary and the United States and north to the Alaska Highway.

They Said It

"We have more demand that we've ever had before in the $175,000 to $200,000 range, with longer waiting lists."
– Porsche dealer Randy Miyagishima, owner of Norden Autohaus, speaking in May 2004.

Bio PETER "PUCK"

Peter Pocklington, aka Peter "Puck," is the nearest thing to a Dickensian capitalist that Edmonton has ever had. Born in London, ON, he earned his business chops by opening two car dealerships there before coming to Edmonton in 1971, where he opened a third. Before long, Pocklington was involved in a number of local businesses, most notably the Edmonton Oilers in 1976 and the Gainer's Packing Plant in 1977.

Pocklington took the Oilers out of the dying World Hockey Association and into the NHL, while adding hockey's greatest all-time player, Wayne Gretzky, to the team in 1979. Fans shelled out a total of $5 million for season tickets before the Oilers' first NHL face-off. Those early moves set the team up for a dynasty that included four Stanley Cup victories between 1984 and 1988. The Oilers dynasty raised the spirits of a city that had suffered economic collapse that same decade.

In 1982, a broke Yugoslavian immigrant named Mirko Petrovic broke into Pocklington's mansion, holding the family hostage for $2 million.

Edmontonians showed their concern by setting up hot dog stands and lawn chairs outside the home as the stand-off unfolded. The crisis finally ended when an officer fired a round at Petrovic, shooting Pocklington first.

Pocklington recovered and launched an unsuccessful bid to lead the federal Progressive Conservatives in 1983, at the same time as his Fidelity Trust Co. was folding. "Puck" then took his first steps towards infamy when, in 1986, staff at Gainer's Packing Plant went on strike. Pocklington shipped in 1,000 workers to take their place.

After six months of picket line violence, a deal was inked, and Pocklington wrangled a multi-million dollar bail-out for the financially troubled Gainer's. He then sold Gretzky to the Los Angeles Kings for $18 million in 1988, and lost Gainer's to the government in 1989 after failing to make scheduled loan payments.

His downhill slide continued. In 1998, he sold the Oilers to local investors, while watching two other businesses — Pocklington Financial Corp. and Hartford Securities — slide into receivership. Most of Pocklington's assets were sold off in bankruptcy sales in 1999. In 2000, Pocklington moved to California.

SMALL BUSINESS

In 2005, 13.6 percent of small businesses (less than 10 employees) in Canada were located in Alberta. In 2005, Alberta's share of Canada's population was 10 percent. (Source: Statistics Canada, Canadian Business Patterns)

- In 2005, 13.6% of small businesses (less than 50 employees) in Canada were located in Alberta. In 2005, Alberta's share of Canada's population was 10%.

PCL Construction Group INC.:
An Edmonton Tradition

PCL Construction (so named after the original Poole Construction Ltd.), is a continent-spanning construction phenomenon and one of Edmonton's first companies. Founded in 1906 by Ernie Poole, the company celebrated its 100th birthday the year after the province celebrated its centennial. In 2006 it had the 20th highest revenue of any business in the province.

Poole's sons, John and George, bought the company from their father in 1948 and grew it until 1977, when they sold it to management. In 2005, the privately-held company posted revenues of $3.3 billion, the 14th highest in the province. The company has residential, institutional and public infrastructure projects spread across North America and into the Bahamas.

John Poole passed away in January 2007, predeceased by his father and brother. Aside from their business acumen, the Poole patriarchs will always be remembered as quiet community benefactors, particularly when it came to arts patronage.

Examples of the Poole legacy includes contributions to the Winspear Centre, the Edmonton Community Foundation, the founding of the annual Alberta Arts Awards and a crucial $5 million contribution towards the reconstruction of the outdated Art Gallery of Alberta (formerly the Edmonton Art Gallery).

Clearly they are emblematic of the Edmonton attitude that it takes more than bricks and mortar to build a great city.

They Said It

"The opportunities are there but it's not automatic that the rising tide raises everybody."

> – Canada West Foundation chief economist Todd Hirsch on a 2006 survey of Edmontonians that found one in three said they haven't benefited from the hot economy.

BUSINESSES IN EDMONTON

The entrepreneurial spirit thrives in Edmonton. In 2006 alone, 28,226 new businesses were incorporated, up 25.3 percent over the previous year.

In 2005, 80,013 businesses called Edmonton home. Of these, 41,578 businesses had employees. The vast majority — 38,982 — of these staffed businesses had fewer than 50 employees while only 127 had more than 500 people on staff.

Source: Edmonton Economic Development Corporation.

COLD FX

Ask an Edmontonian what they do to stay healthy during winter and they'll probably tell you one of two things. One, they get a flu shot, or two, they stock up on "Cold-fX," a locally-invented, ginseng-based cold remedy and prevention regime.

The product was co-invented by the late Dr. Peter Pang and Dr. Jacqueline Sharp, who is now CEO of Edmonton's CV Technologies, which produces the unique pharmaceutical. The product has undergone seven clinical trials and finally, in February 2007, earned Health Canada approval of claims that Cold-fX can "reduce the frequency, severity, and duration of cold and flu symptoms by boosting the immune system."

Did you know...

that all change tossed into fountains in West Edmonton Mall goes to charity?

GET YOUR GEEK GAME ON

You can't have a conversation about economic diversification in Edmonton without mentioning BioWare Corp. Founded in 1995 by CEOs Dr. Ray Muzyka and Dr. Greg Zeschuk, Bioware today boasts a library of 13 multiplayer, sci-fi and fantasy video game titles, including international hits like Star Wars: Knights of the Old Republic, which sold three million copies and has been ranked the 26th most popular game of all time. Other top titles include the wildly popular Baldur's Gate series.

The hyper-educated pair of programmers leveraged their early medical pay cheques to be their own venture capitalists. By 1996, their gamble already started to pay dividends with the success of their first title, Shattered Steel, and by 2000, the pair left their scrubs and clipboards behind for good. In 2006, the company had estimated earnings of $20 million.

DOWNTOWN EDMONTON

- Number of people who work downtown: 60,000
- Number who live there: 13,000
- Number who study there: 20,000
- Number of specialty and department stores downtown: 425
- Number of kilometres of climate controlled pedways: 13
- Number of parking facilities: 85
- Number of parking spaces: 45,000+

Source: Edmonton Economic Development Corporation; Edmonton Downtown Business Association.

EDMONTON'S FIVE RICHEST NEIGHBOURHOODS

	Avg Household Income	Number of Households
Quesnell Heights	$216,773	120
Rhatigan Ridge	$156,073	1,210
Henderson Estates	$156,010	530
Ogilvie Ridge	$151,288	495
Westbrook Estate	$150,245	470

HOME PRICES

Edmonton residential resale prices and sales volumes broke all records in 2006, and Edmonton became one of the last Canadian markets to record "booming" prices as other major urban centres saw the market flatten out.

As of December 2006, the average single family home was selling for $341,933, up 51.9 percent from 2005, and the average price for a condominium unit rocketed from $149,254 to $227,428. In 2006, a total of 21,984 homes were sold at an average price of $292,829.

The Katz Group:
Edmonton's Biggest Corporation

If you've bought drugs in Canada, it was probably at a Katz Group store. The pharmaceutical retail group is the moving force behind the IDA and Guardian drugstores, Pharmaplus Drugmart, Rexall Drug Stores, Medicine Shoppe Pharmacies, Herbies for Drug and Food, Meditrust mail-order pharmacies, Snyders Drug Stores in the United States, and Propharm Ltd. All told, The Katz Group runs over 1,800 drug stores across North America, with approximately 15,000 employees.

And, unsurprisingly, that makes the company Edmonton's biggest corporation and Alberta's largest private corporation. A greater surprise might come from the revelation that, with revenues of $6.5 billion in 2005, the company outperformed even oil sands giant Syncrude Canada, which posted revenues of $5.86 billion the same year. The company is 100 per cent owned by Daryl Katz, a 45 year-old University of Alberta alumnus who in 2006 was ranked the 486th richest man in the world by Forbes magazine. According to the magazine's rankings, Katz' net worth is $1.9 billion, making him the 12th richest man in Canada, and the country's second youngest billionaire.

Nationally, the average price in 2006 was $276,974.

Source: Edmonton Real Estate Board; CBC; Canada Mortgage and Housing Corporation.

UP AND UP

In Edmonton, where the threshold is $500,000, 144 luxury homes have sold IN 2006, a 177 per cent increase over this time last year. The most expensive sale was $1.6 million.

RENTING

Average Rent ($ Dollars)

City	1 bedroom	2 bedrooms
Montreal	562	616
Edmonton	608	732
Calgary	666	808
Ottawa	762	920
Vancouver	788	1,004
Toronto	888	1,052

Source: Canada Mortgage and Housing Corporation.

EDMONTON'S FIVE POOREST NEIGHBOURHOODS

	Avg Household Income	Number of Households
Central McDougall	$26,302	2,615
Boyle Street	$31,429	2,855
Cromdale	$32,105	1,090
Queen Mary Park	$32,597	3,600
Westwood	$32,732	1,715

Source: City of Edmonton.

GETTING TO WORK

- Edmonton worker's usual mode of transportation to work is as a driver or passenger in a vehicle.
- Percentage that drive or passenger in vehicle: 84.3
- Public Transportation: 8.6
- Walk: 4.7
- Bicycle: 1.2

LENGTH OF COMMUTE

Percentage of workers commuted between 5 km and 15 km: 56

Percenage who commuted more than 25 km: 9

- Percentage who travel less than 5 km: · 33.7%
- Between 5 and 14.9 km: 46.3
- Between 15 and 24.9 km: 10.9

Source: OMA Canada; Statistics Canada.

HOW EDMONTONIANS GET TO WORK

- Drive a motor vehicle   246,820
- Passenger in a motor vehicle   22,825
- Public Transit   38,140
- Walk or cycle   22,155
- Other   3,965

Did you know...

that the GDP per capita of people living in the Calgary/Edmonton corridor is ten percent higher than the U.S. metropolitan area average, according to a TD Bank report.

EMPLOYMENT

Edmonton's top employers are in sales and service occupations. In 2005, they were responsible for about 144,769 Edmontonian pay cheques. Another 109,502 of us are employed in business finance and administration occupations. Trades, transport and equipment operators, and related occupations are the third largest area of employment.

The city also has the curse of having far too many managers — 63,149 to be exact — rounding out the fourth largest occupation area. The fifth biggest employment sector in 2005 was the category that includes "occupations in social science, education, government service and religion," which kept 44,559 Edmontonians in groceries.

GENDER GAP

Women earn an average $17.73 an hour, 75 percent of the $23.76 earned by men.

Source: Alberta Human Resources and Employment; Statistics Canada.

OIL AND GAS

Not surprisingly, one of Edmonton's top areas of manufacture is in the production of oil, gas and petrochemicals. In all, approximately 15,000 Edmontonians work in the manufacture of these goods.

Did you know...

that Edmonton is second in terms of projected Gross Metropolitan Product (GMP) growth among Canada's 20 major metropolises, according to a report published by the Conference Board of Canada.

ADDING TO THE COFFERS

Every tick upward in the price of oil further stokes an already heated Edmonton and Alberta economy. Provincial revenues increase by $65 million for every dollar increase in the price of oil, and oil royalty revenue now accounts for almost thirty percent of the provincial budget.

The impact of the gas and oil industry is felt in every aspect of life in the city. It has fuelled the current construction boom and given the city a sense optimism that is unparalled anywhere else in the country.

OIL SANDS

Size of the proven oil reserves, in barrels, of Saudia Arabia: 262 billion
Size of the oil in the underground deposits known collectively as the tarsands around the area of Fort McMurray, the largest lode of hydrocarbons in the world: 1.6 trillion

- Number of barrels considered recoverable with current technology: 174 billion
- Number of barrels considered recoverable with emerging, but not yet established technology: 311 billion
- Number of barrels a day Alberta produces today: 1.594 million
- Number of those that are from the oil sands: 964,000
- Number from conventional sources: 630,000
- Cost to recover is $7 versus 12

Source: Alberta Ministry of Energy.

CANADA CALLING

- Percentage of Canada's oil production accounted for by Alberta, according to the Canadian Association of Petroleum Producers: 72
- Percentage of Canada's natural gas production accounted for by Alberta: 78

CAPITAL CASE
- Total capital expenditures in Alberta's oil and gas sector as of 2006: $32.9 billion
- Total capital expenditures in Alberta's non-energy sector as of 2006: $18 billion

CASH REGISTER
- Total revenue from non-renewable resources to the Alberta government in fiscal year 2000-01: $10.586 billion
- Actual amount in 2005-2006, double what it was two years ago, and five times what it was in the 1990s: $14.6 billion

WHAT TO DO
Responding to the question of what the government should do with unexpected oil revenues of $7 billion, percentage of Albertans who said spend the money on improving existing government programs and services, according to a survey done for the Canada West Foundation: 37
- Percentage who said divide up the money and give it to individual Albertans: 14

MAJOR CITY PROJECTS
As of October 2006, Edmonton's major projects are worth an estimated $30 billion. Of this, 68 percent will be generated by oil, gas and oil sands, the top income-generating project.

Weblinks

Edmonton Economic Development Corporation
http://www.edmonton.com/eedc/page.asp?page=97
Cruise this site for info on any imaginable aspect of Edmonton economy.

Edmonton Chamber of Commerce
www.edmontonchamber.com/
Committed to "create the best possible environment for business," this site offers valuable information about the business scene in Edmonton.

Jobs in Canada (Edmonton)
jobsincanada.com/index.asp?pageid=32&component=content&item=32
Want to find a job in Edmonton? Start here!

Politics

POLITICAL BEGINNINGS

In 1795, the first vestiges of European settlement in the Edmonton area were a pair of competing fur trading posts on the banks of the North Saskatchewan River — Edmonton House, owned by Hudson's Bay Co. (HBC), and Augustus House, controlled by the competing North West Company.

By 1830, the two posts amalgamated into a single HBC post called Fort Edmonton, under the direction of George Simpson. The site is now the location of Alberta's provincial Legislature.

In those early years, small settler communities formed near the Fort on the north and south sides of the river, but local political leadership was nonexistent. It was not until 1870, when the Dominion of Canada officially purchased Rupert's Land from the HBC, that conditions were ripe for the creation of proper governance — a development aided by the 1874 arrival of the North West Mounted Police.

In 1892, Edmonton was incorporated as a town. The first mayor, Matthew McCauley, rapidly established the town's first school board and Board of Trade (later to become the Chamber of Commerce) and the precursors of a municipal police service.

Mayor McCauley was well-connected with the federal Liberals and this tie enabled Edmonton to maintain political prominence over Strathcona, a competing town on the south bank of the North Saskatchewan River.

Edmonton was incorporated as a city in 1904, and in 1905 became the capital city of the new province of Alberta.

MUNICIPAL REPRESENTATION

Edmontonians are represented by a mayor and 12 councillors — two from each of the six city "wards." This system was introduced in 1971 to ensure that every city region was equally represented by city council.

Today, councillors complain that their rapidly expanding ward populations are too large to govern effectively. In 2006, Council discussed the addition of a new ward to reduce the number of constituents per councillor from 59,000 to 50,000. The council, however, decided to stay with the present system and, recognizing the ever-increasing difficulty of their jobs, voted themselves a 13 percent wage increase.

THE HIGH COST OF GOVERNMENT

It costs $1.8 billion to run the city of Edmonton for a year, the single biggest expense being its bus and light rail transit service which cost a whopping $228 million in 2006.

- Amount spent on police services: $207 million
- Drainage: $181 million
- Municipal fleet and buildings: $182 million
- Parks: $177 million
- Fire and ambulance service: $142 million
- Roads: $242 million
- Snow removal: $34.5 million
- Waste management: $77.3 million
- Libraries: $38 million

Source: City of Edmonton.

Did you know...

that the 1995 civic election cost the city of Edmonton $918,000?

Did you know...

that since 1952, Edmonton's municipal elections have been held on the third Monday of October?

Edmonton's Most Outrageous Mayor

Edmonton's first Ukrainian mayor holds the distinction of being the city's most infamous. William Hawrelak was first appointed mayor in 1951, when Sydney Parsons left office due to illness. Later that year, he defeated Parsons in an election.

Hawrelak remained in office until a 1959 inquiry by the Supreme Court of Alberta found him guilty of "gross misconduct" in a number of land transactions. In one case, Hawrelak used inside information to sell a supermarket developer some land that he owned a half-interest in. Not only that, he obtained that interest for a song by assuring the original landowner that a shopping development would not be located on the land. The investigation into this and other land deals forced Hawrelak to resign and cost him $100,000 when he had to pay an out of court settlement to the city.

Despite his fall from grace, Hawrelak's charm and his strong record of municipal development — the Stanley Milner library, Edmonton Zoo, Royal Alexandra Hospital, Groat Bridge, Yellowhead freeway and four major city parks were all built during his reign — allowed him to regroup and reclaim his position as mayor in 1963.

But alas, Hawrelak had apparently not learned his lesson and in 1965 another shady land transaction and another court decision again forced him from office. Then this comeback kid did it again.

In 1974, he again found his way into the Mayor's office, but not for long. This time his downfall would not be his penchant for questionable business deals — his heart was the culprit. In late 1975, Hawrelak died of a heart attack.

Public opinion surrounding Hawrelak remains split between those who praise his mayoral accomplishments and those who think him a crook. Those Edmontonians of the latter persuasion and who have a long municipal memory, to this day refuse to acknowledge Hawrelak Park, instead favouring its original name, Mayfair Park.

CITY DEBT

Led by former Mayor Bill Smith, Edmonton City Council refused to borrow money throughout the 1990s.

Recognizing that the city was in need of major transportation improvements, in 2002 Edmonton City Council shelved the no debt policy and embarked on a five-year plan allowing the borrowing of up to $50 million dollars to combat the so-called "infrastructure debt."

PROPERTY TAXES

Based on a sample house as defined as a 25 to 30 year-old detached 3-bedroom bungalow with a main floor area of 1,200 square feet, finished full basement and a double car garage, on a 6,000 square foot lot. Utility charges include telephones, power, water, sewer, land drainage and garbage collection.

Ottawa	$4,659
Toronto	$4,624
Saskatoon	$4,487
Vancouver	$4,216
Regina	$4,184
St. John's	$4,082
Edmonton	**$3889**
Calgary	$3708
Fredericton	$3, 694
Montreal	$3,644
Winnipeg	$3,577
Halifax	$3,402

Source: City of Edmonton

Did you know...

that in 1936, Edmonton aldermen were paid $500 a year?

Bio EMILY MURPHY

Emily Murphy was born in Ontario in 1868 but settled with her family in Edmonton in 1907. Murphy's career in Edmonton was a catalyst for the actions of the Famous Five. An agitator for the political rights of women, she was a key figure in the successful lobby for the Dower Act of 1911, which for the first time guaranteed divorced women a one-third share of the family property. In 1916, she made history again, becoming the first female police magistrate in the entire British Empire.

Murphy's new power brought with it her greatest challenge: on her first day working as a judge, a lawyer asserted that women were not recognized as "persons" under the British North America Act (BNA), and that she, therefore, had no jurisdiction over the court. Other lawyers repeated this challenge. Prime Minister Robert Borden also refused to accept her candidacy for the Senate on the same grounds that women were not considered "persons."

Murphy would have none of it. For twelve years she dedicated herself to the fight to have women declared "persons." A shrewd political mind, Murphy found a clause of the Supreme Court Act that stipulated that any five interested persons could petition the Supreme Court for a ruling on a point of Constitutional Law.

Murphy chose her four Albertan allies: Nellie McClung, Louise McKinney, Henrietta Edwards and Irene Parlby. The quintuplet collected an amazing 500,000 signatures from across Canada in their Supreme Court challenge. In 1928, they were disheartened when the Supreme Court ruled against them. They appealed the decision to the Judicial Committee of the Privy Council in London, England and they won. On October 18, 1929, the Privy Council ruled that women were, in fact, legal "persons" under the BNA Act.

Edmonton Mayors

Term	Name	Profession
1892-1894	Matthew McCauley	Farmer
1895-1896	H. Charles Wilson	Doctor, pharmacist
1896	Cornelius Gallagher	Meat packer
1897	John A. McDougall	Wholesale, retail, and insurance seller
1898-1899	William. S. Edmiston	Architect
1900-1901	Kenneth W. MacKenzie	School teacher, principal
1906	Charles May	Construction contractor
1907	William A. Griesbach	Lawyer, soldier
1908	John A. McDougall	Wholesale, retail and insurance seller
1909-1910	Robert Lee	Mining, timber, real estate, insurance
1911-1912	G.S. Armstrong	Postmaster
1913	William Short	Lawyer
1914	William J. McNamara	Land developer
1914-1917	William T. Henry	Farmer, retailer
1918	Harry M. E. Evans	Bonds, insurance, real estate dealer
1919-1920	Joseph A. Clarke	Lawyer
1921-1923	David M. Duggan	Financial services provider
1924-1926	Kenneth A. Blatchford	Insurance broker
1927-1929	Ambrose U.G. Bury	Lawyer, judge
1930-1931	James M. Douglas	Mercantile businessman
1932-1934	Daniel K. Knott	Press operator

Term	Name	Profession
1935-1937	Joseph A. Clarke	Lawyer
1938-1945	John W. Fry	Real estate dealer, contractor
1946-1949	Harry D. Ainlay	School teacher, principal
1950-1951	Sidney Parsons	Contractor, tradesman
1952-1959	William Hawrelak	Businessman, developer
1959	Frederick J. Mitchell	Minerals prospector, tennis pro
1960-1963	Elmer E. Roper	Pressman
1964-1965	William Hawrelak	Businessman, developer
1965-1968	Vincent M. Dantzer	Airforce officer, economist, lawyer
1968-1974	Ivor G. Dent	Teacher, principal
1974-1975	William Hawrelak	Businessman, developer
1975-1977	Terry J. Cavanagh	Manager, public relations officer, hockey player
1977-1983	Cecil J. Purves	Businessman
1983-1988	Laurence Decore	Lawyer, developer
1988-1989	Terry J. Cavanagh	Manager, public relations officer, hockey player
1989-1995	Janice Reimer	Politician, community activist
1995-2004	Bill Smith	Football player, business owner
2004-	Mandel, Stephen	Businessman, real estate developer

Source: Edmonton Public Library.

Mark Lisac is an Edmonton writer. He is also the publisher and edi-tor of *Insight into Government*, a weekly newsletter on Alberta pol-itics. Of the scandals he has the following insight: "They make a curious collection. Edmonton's scandals have generally gone unproved, unexplained and, when they have been proven and explained, have been forgiven by the public." And they say Calgary has a unique political culture!

1. Frank Oliver's land politics
The founding editor of the *Edmonton Bulletin*, later federal minister of the interior in Wilfrid Laurier's governments, was instrumental in agitation in the late 1880s to remove the Papaschase Indian band from a reserve it had taken in 1877 on nearly 40 square miles of land in what later became south Edmonton. Most of the 200-plus members of the band were either reclassified as belonging to anoth-er group of Indians or induced to take scrip for other lands by the late 1880s. The reserve is generally agreed to have taken in land south of what is now 51st Avenue, between 17th and 119th Streets. There's still disagreement on what happened and exactly what land was involved.

2. The McMillan Affair
Sex and politics! Premier John Brownlee resigned in 1934 after being sued under the province's Seduction Act by the father of Vivian McMillan, an 18-year-old government stenographer he allegedly seduced. A sensational and lurid court case and various appeals all the way up to Britain's Privy Council were complicated. A satisfactory version of the truth never came out and there were reasons to doubt McMillan's story. McMillan eventually moved to the U.S., dying in obscurity decades later, while Brownlee became a highly respected Edmonton lawyer. The province repealed the Seduction Act in the 1980s.

3. Bill Hawrelak's real estate

Hawrelak was a popular mayor whose real estate deals on the side crossed motel owner and alderman Ed Leger. Leger, angry about next-door competition he was told would never appear, found that Hawrelak's brother-in law had bought city land on the site and that others in Hawrelak's family were involved in city land deals. A judicial investigation found Hawrelak guilty of gross misconduct and he resigned. He was elected again in 1963 and forced out of office again after complaints about his interest in land sold to the city. Voters elected him a third time in 1974; he died of a heart attack within a year.

4. The ATB-WEM loan

The provincial government-owned Alberta Treasury Branches agreed in 1994 to a $420-million refinancing of West Edmonton Mall. The deal led to a number of accusations, including bribery and political interference. It was featured in a privately published book titled *Banksters and Prairie Boys*, which sold more than 10,000 copies but was never discussed by any of the parties named in it. Lawsuits related to the deal ended with a settlement accepted in a 20-minute court hearing in 2002. All parties agreed never to talk about anything related to the lawsuits and they never did.

5. The Principal Group

Locally famous businessman Donald Cormie presided over an investment empire that crashed in 1987, costing thousands of investors scores of millions of dollars. A court-ordered investigation found the companies had not really been profitable for years and that the Alberta government had willfully refused to regulate the company effectively. But a satisfactory explanation of what really happened inside the government never emerged. The province reimbursed investors much of the lost money. People who followed the story were entertained by soap-opera details of a romantic relationship between Cormie and a woman on his staff.

POLITICAL GAINS FOR WOMEN

1885: Unmarried women property owners gain the right to vote and hold office in school matters across the province.

1916: The Alberta Equal Suffrage Act gives women 'absolute equality' with men in provincial, municipal and school affairs, allowing them to vote and run for office in all Alberta-based elections.

1918: The Canada Elections Act gives all women over 21 the federal vote.

Bio PRESTON MANNING

Geeky glasses, a 50s style haircut and a twangy speaking voice hardly seems the description of a political tour de force. But with this awkward recipe, Edmontonian Preston Manning paved the way for one of the biggest political upsets of the Canadian political establishment.

Born Ernest Preston Manning in 1942 in Edmonton, the young politician-to-be graduated from the University of Alberta in 1964, and then mounted an unsuccessful bid for a Social Credit seat in the 1965 federal election. Undaunted by this early failure, the young Manning immediately blazed a brave trail, going to work for his dad, Social Credit Premier Ernest Manning, researching a book, developing a policy for the provincial government, and building up his political acumen.

The "small c" conservative Manning revived the right-wing of politics. In 1987, Manning spearheaded the creation of the Reform Party, built on a platform of fiscal responsibility, provincial equality and parliamentary reform. In the 1988 election, the Reform Party did poorly – no reform MPs, not even Manning, were elected.

By 1993, however, the Canadian political tide had changed. Progressive Conservative Prime Minister Brian Mulroney had left his party in shambles and Manning's Reform Party reaped the reward,

1922: Izena Ross, Edmonton's first female alderperson, is elected.

1933: Margaret Crang, the city's second female alderman, and at 23 the youngest alderman, is elected to council.

1941: Edmonton's Cora Casselman is the first female Liberal elected to the House of Commons.

1989: Jan Reimer is elected the first woman mayor of Edmonton

winning an amazing 52 seats. Four years later, the Reform Party secured 60 seats and official opposition status.

The Reform Party was, however, not without problems. Although it was strong in the west, the Party had no seats east of Ontario. Keenly aware of this problem, in 1998 Manning initiated the United Alternative movement aimed at merging the Reform Party with the Progressive Conservative Party in a bid to establish an eastern base of support.

By 2000, the Canadian Alliance Party was born. Manning resigned as Leader of the Official Opposition to run for the leadership of the new Canadian Alliance Party but lost to Stockwell Day. That same year, Manning revealed that he was being treated for prostate cancer and in 2001 he left federal politics.

Since his political retirement, Manning has set up the Manning Centre for Freedom and Democracy, a conservative think-tank, and in 2006 dabbled his toe in provincial politics by hinting at a possible run at replacing Premier Ralph Klein as Alberta's Progressive Conservative leader. Unknown forces kept Manning from running, even though a newspaper poll showed he had far greater public support than any of the front-running candidates.

MUNICIPAL ELECTION TURN OUTS (PERCENTAGE)

1893	47.7
1905	52.3
1915	40.2
1925	43.3
1935	41.6
1945	28.0
1955	11.2
1966	59.2
1974	48.0
1986	33.8
1995	49.7
2004	41.8

Source: Edmonton Public Library

THE PROVINCIAL SCENE

Edmonton has 18 provincial government ridings. Provincially, Edmontonians are known for their varied political allegiances. While provincial political tastes in the rest of the province have tended to the conservatives (whether Progressive Conservative or Social Credit), Edmontonians have displayed a penchant for the New Democrat and Liberal parties.

Did you know...

that Edmonton's lowest ever turnout for a municipal election occurred in 1956, with just 13,360 people, or 10 percent of eligible voters turning up at the ballot? The election returned Mayor Hawrelak to office for his second term.

They Said It

"Over the years I have been portrayed by newsmen and commentators as an enigma –reserved, dour, cold and void of emotions. I am happy to report to you than none of these afflictions have ever caused me any pain."

– **Ernest Manning**

They Said It

"I do not want to pull through life like a thread that has no knot. I want to leave something behind when I go; some small legacy of truth, some word that will shine in a dark place."

– **Nellie McClung, one of the Famous Five**

SOCIAL CREDIT'S EDMONTON CONNECTION

The Social Credit party was officially a product of Calgary and rural Alberta's political climate, but Edmonton extended its life. Edmontonian Premier Ernest C. Manning led the So-Creds from 1943 to 1968, winning seven successive elections. Manning shored up support for his party across the province with a radio program called "Back to the Bible Hour," broadcast from the Paramount Theatre in downtown Edmonton.

Source: University of British Columbia Library; Legislative Assembly of Alberta website.

Did you know...

that City council changed the title "alderman" to the gender-neutral "councillor" in 1995? Activist council members Tooker Gomberg, and Michael Phair (Alberta's first and so far only "out" gay politician), were the first to use the term.

SOCIAL CREDIT

As appealing as aspects of the social credit message were in the hard times of the Great Depression, elements of the party's philosophy were unnerving. In 1935, Social Creditors Joseph Unwin and George Powell published over 6,000 leaflets which likened a list of prominent Albertans as insects to be "exterminated."

It is doubtful that the hyperbolic writers intended their message to be taken literally, but the extreme language would not be tolerated. One of the men identified in the leaflets was Major General William Griesbach, who turned out to be more of a lion than a bug. Griesbach charged the perpetrators with libel and counseling murder. The latter charge was eventually dropped, but Unwin and Powell were found guilty of libel and sentenced to a short period of hard labour.

Did you know...

that on April 25, 1906, a motion was made in the legislature to move the capital of Alberta from Edmonton to Calgary? It was defeated.

EDMONTON FIGHTS SOCIAL CREDIT CENSORSHIP

In 1937, the Social Credit Party introduced the Accurate News and Information Act - legislation that would have required newspapers to print, upon demand, government-authored "corrections" of newspaper stories. The act also sought to strip newspapers of the right to anonymous sources and required them to suspend publication upon government orders.

The *Edmonton Journal* didn't take this attack on the press lying down. The newspaper penned editorials railing against Aberhart's plan to reign in the press. Aberhart, they wrote, "must not deny to others the very freedom of speech and action that permitted him to secure the post from which now he looks down upon the common reporter as a public nuisance."

In 1938, Canada's Supreme Court sided with the Journal and struck down Aberhart's "press act." Later that year, the *Edmonton Journal* was given a Pulitzer Prize for its defence of press freedoms – the first ever given to a non-American newspaper.

Source: Alberta, Aberhart, and Social Credit; University of British Columbia Library.

THE FEDERAL SCENE

Edmonton is home to eight federal electoral districts. Generally, since the 1950s Edmontonians have favoured conservative parties in Ottawa — from the Progressive Conservatives, to Reform, to the Alliance and the Conservatives. In total, Edmonton Liberal candidates have been elected to Parliament only 12 times in federal elections from 1953 to 2006. The NDP managed one victory in the same period.

Did you know...

that the highest recorded rate of voter turn out in a municipal election occurred in 1918? That year, 83.5 percent of Edmontonians turned out to vote for mayor and council.

INDIAN ASSOCIATION OF ALBERTA

One of Canada's most important political organizations is the Indian Association of Alberta (IAA). First established in 1933 as the League of Indians of Alberta and renamed the IAA in 1939, it was founded by Native leaders who saw in Canada a great need for political reform to alter Canada's offensive Indian policy. It has always been based in Edmonton. Since its founding, the IAA has championed political issues important to the province's First People as it has lobbied provincial and federal governments and sought to educate the public. In the aftermath of the infamous 1969 White Paper it was the IAA that became the "voice" of Native Canadians who opposed the federal plan to discontinue Natives' special status. The path of the IAA has never been an easy one. It has constantly fought for funding and in the late 1990s faced the loss of both federal and provincial support. Despite this blow, the IAA remains one of the most active and important advocate groups for Native rights in Alberta and, indeed, across the country.

"REDMONTON"

Depending on your political persuasion, the nickname "Redmonton" refers either to the city's support of leftist labour-oriented politicians ("Red" being short for "Communist"), or its tendency to support the centre-left Liberal party, provincially or federally.

Although the nickname overstates the power of the left in Edmonton, it is a fitting description for a city that has bucked the overwhelmingly rightist tendencies of provincial politics.

In 1919, the *Edmonton Free Press* was founded to counter the anti-labour sentiment found in both the *Edmonton Journal* and *Edmonton Bulletin*. That year nearly all unionized employees in the city joined in a month-long solidarity strike with Winnipeg workers. The then-mayor, "Fighting" Joe Clarke, refused to break the strike, presumably to avoid the violence and chaos seen in Winnipeg.

From 1922 until 1962, Labour-oriented city council members were regularly elected, including the three mayors Stanley Milner, Sidney

Parsons and Elmer Roper. Labour power declined sharply from the 1960s onwards, but left-of-centre opinion remained in Edmonton, supporting both the New Democrats and Liberals in the Legislature (although both parties have been relegated to perpetual opposition status).

Weblinks

City of Edmonton

www.edmonton.ca/portal/server.pt
For information on all things related to the city government — the ward system, councillor bios and all about the mayor's office — follow the appropriate links on this site.

Provincial Reps

www.assembly.ab.ca/net/index.aspx?p=mla_csv
Find out what you need to know about city MLAs using this site maintained by the Alberta Assembly.

Edmonton Politics, 101

www.foundlocally.com/Edmonton/Local/Government.htm
Use foundlocally.com to link to information of all sorts concerning political representation of all stripes and persuasions in Edmonton.

Then and Now

When Edmonton was first settled by people of European descent in the late 1700s, it was little more than a couple of fur trade forts — Fort Edmonton and Fort Augustus — controlled by the Hudson's Bay Company. It would, however, be nearly another 100 years, until 1871, before a bona fide village by the name of Edmonton was born.

POPULATION, THEN AND NOW

1878	148
1887	350
1899	2,212
1911	24,900
1921	58,821
1931	79,059
1941	93,924
1951	158,092
1961	276,018
1971	436,264
1981	521,205
1991	614,655

| 2001 | 666,104 |
| 2005 | 712,391 |

Source: City of Edmonton.

STRATHCONA

Edmonton's south side neighborhood, Old Strathcona, has undergone many changes since its inception as "South Edmonton." This site, the terminus of the Calgary and Edmonton Railway, was originally earmarked to be groomed as a commercial centre that would soon eclipse Edmonton.

By June 1899, the community of 1,156 was incorporated as a town named after Hudson's Bay Governor, railroad magnate, MP and Canadian High Commissioner, Donald A. Smith, Lord Strathcona. Initially, Strathcona prospered, living up to its billing. In March 1907, with a population of 2,500, it was elevated to city status.

In 1912, however, Strathcona's fortunes turned. That year, the city of 5,579 decided to amalgamate with Edmonton, population 24,900. This would prove a fateful decision. After amalgamation, Strathcona entered a period of economic depression. Indeed, the area did not fully recover until the 1980s when the appeal of its turn-of-the-century buildings, a thriving theatre industry and student culture revitalized the area.

UKRAINIAN CAPITAL OF CANADA

After Confederation, the Canadian government set to work settling the west. It got off to a slow start and by 1890, western Canada was home to just two percent of Canada's population. To encourage more settlement, the federal government distributed millions of pamphlets around the globe, boasting of the riches to be found in the Canadian west. This paid off, and by World War I over one million immigrants from all over the world, lured by promises of fertile lands and warm weather, settled in western Canada.

In 1891, immigrants Ivan Pylypow and Wasyl Eleniak made histo-

They Said It

"It will surprise many who kick at the Galacians [Ukrainians] that those who came in only three years ago have from 30 to 70 acres cultivated. Give them time."

– The Edmonton Bulletin, July 22, 1897

ry as the first Ukrainians to arrive in Alberta. Both settled north of Edmonton and like them, most Ukrainian immigrants at first established rurally. Over time, however, Edmonton became an urban mecca for the Ukrainian arrivals and the city became home to the largest Ukrainian community outside of Ukraine.

In 1911, the Ukrainian newspaper, *Nova Hromada* was published and in 1928 *Ukraïns'ki visti/Ukrainian News* first appeared and has been published ever since. Ukrainians have also made a mark on the politics of the city. Two of its mayors, William Hawrelak and Laurence Decore, came from Ukrainian heritage. In 2001, Edmonton's Ukrainian population numbered 125,720 — by far the largest in Canada.

WAR MEASURES

Life in Canada was not always easy for transplanted Ukrainians. The War Measures Act enacted in WWI enabled the Canadian government to intern more than 5,000 Ukrainians as "enemy aliens." Ukrainian men, women and children were forced to work in labour camps across the country and were compelled to stay there for two years after the war ended.

Today there is a movement afoot in the House of Commons to pass Bill C-331, the Ukrainian Canadian Recognition and Restitution Act, an acknowledgment of the injustices of the internment and an effort to redress this distressing chapter in Canadian history.

BLACK AND WHITE

Despite its need of settlers, Edmonton did not welcome everyone. When a group of Black settlers arrived in 1910-11, the Edmonton Board of Trade, the Imperial Order of Daughters of the Empire and the Edmonton Trades and Labour Council all petitioned to have them barred.

Federal Minister of the Interior, Edmonton's Liberal MP Frank Oliver, joined the petition and in May 1911 recommended to the

Gateway to the North

Edmonton lies 300 km north of Calgary in the fertile North Saskatchewan River Valley. Covering an area larger than Chicago, Philadelphia, Toronto or Montreal, Edmonton boasts one of the lowest population densities of any city on the continent.

The first inhabitants, local First Nations, gathered in the area about 12,000 years ago when an ice-free corridor emerged and timber, water and wildlife became available in the region. The area changed forever when, in 1754, Anthony Henday, a European explorer working for the Hudson's Bay Company (HBC), entered the Edmonton area, ushering in an era that would see the establishment of a series of trading posts.

In 1821, when the North West and HBC amalgamated (under the HBC flag), Edmonton became the region's fur trading hub. The fertile land there attracted settlers in droves and Edmonton became not just the lynchpin of the western fur trade, but a major commercial and agricultural centre.

At the end of the 19th century, as the epidemic of gold fever raged, would-be prospectors en route to the Klondike made Edmonton their northern gateway to gold. In 1904, Edmonton, then a community of 8,350, incorporated. A year later, it became the capital city of the new province of Alberta.

Edmonton's role as the "Gateway to the North" continued in 1929 when it became home to Canada's first licensed airfield and

Governor General that "any immigrants belonging to the Negro race, which race is deemed unsuitable to the climate and requirements of Canada" be prohibited from taking up residence.

For unknown reasons, Oliver's proposal never saw the light of day, and he and the rest of the Laurier Liberals were voted out of office in the fall of 1911. Before leaving government, however, Oliver managed with the Immigration Act of 1910 to tack a $200 landing fee on new Canadians of "Asiatic" descent.

became the distribution centre for mail, food and medical supplies destined for the Canadian North. World War II saw Edmonton play another important role in Canada's northward infrastructure as the city became the base for the construction of the Alaska Highway and the Northwest Staging Route.

Edmonton's destiny took another direction when Imperial Oil struck it rich at nearby Leduc in 1947. With the discoveries of significant oil reserves, Edmonton became the headquarters of Alberta's lucrative oil industry. The population soared — a population of 269,000 in 1960 grew to 521,000 by 1981.

Oil brought incredible wealth, but in the 1980s and 1990s it also brought financial hardship. The introduction of the 1981 National Energy Program, the 1986 collapse of world oil prices and massive government cutbacks sent the city into a slump.

Indeed, Edmonton's fortunes did not make a full recovery until the late 1990s when economic diversification and resurgence in the world oil market gave the city a much-needed boost.

Since then, renewed prosperity has ushered in an era of immigration to the city as Canadians and people from around the globe, like their 19th century predecessors, see in Edmonton a vast potential for prosperity. If current forecasts hold true, 83,000 new residents will move to Edmonton between 2006 and 2010.

DESPERATION OF THE DIRTY 30S

During the recession and western drought of the 1930s, Edmontonians were desperate for food, desperate for work and desperate for hope. About 15 percent of the population was on relief, but that did not count single males, those who were too proud to collect it or those who were ineligible because they were not Canadian citizens.

On December 20, 1932, citizens banded together to do what they could to ease the situation. Approximately 10,000 Edmontonians planned to gather at City Hall and from there, to march on the provincial legislature to protest against worsening unemployment.

The so-called "Hunger March" was declared illegal by the United Farmers of Alberta (UFA) government, who called out the police to deal with the discontented crowd. Things quickly got out of hand, and mounted police were soon attacking unarmed protesters with truncheons. The affair looked bad for UFA and hastened its eventual demise.

As for the desperate Edmontonians, they, like all Canadians, would have to wait out the depression until WWII revitalized the economy.

Did you know...

that in the booming days following the Leduc strike, oil rig workers worked a standard eight-hour day, perched atop a derrick, and they did so seven days a week, for months on end?

Take 5 JENNIE VISSER'S FIVE MEMORIES OF GROWING UP IN EDMONTON

Jennie (Nicolai) Visser has lived in Edmonton and area for over 70 years. Her husband Clarence Visser came to Edmonton from Holland in 1947. Together they have lived on a farm at the northeast edge of the city for 56 years. The farm was annexed to the city in 1982. Children and grandchildren now also live on the same land, which continues to be used as a market garden.

1. **Walking through the Hudson Bay Reserve.** Located north of the Royal Alexandra Hospital, it was then a big open space where you could hear the songs of the meadowlark.

2. **Picnicking near an ever-running spring of clear,** clean water. Just across the Dawson Bridge near a coal mine, the spot is now part of a golf course.

3. **Traveling by streetcar.** For five cents, we could ride the streetcars all over the city. Crossing the High Level Bridge was always exciting.

4. **Being quarantined.** I don't remember ever being ill during my pre-school days in Saskatchewan, but in Edmonton we broke out with many contagious diseases and were quarantined with door signs for measles, chicken pox, mumps and scarlet fever. Many days we missed school, and I spent a long stretch in the Royal Alexandra Hospital.

5. **Front yard gardens.** Always there were gardens. Most people's front lawns were covered with potatoes. Dad delivered many vegetables to help pay for my hospital stay—and that was pre-Medicare. His garden was his life of neighbourliness. When he became ill in the '80s, his big concern was who would tend his beloved garden. Today a grandson living in his house in the Norwood district keeps a well-tended garden.

GETTING 'ROUND, THEN AND NOW

In the 1890s, the Edmonton Bus Line ferried people by train around the city. Between 1908 and 1913, a funicular railway — a cable operated tram — traversed the steep hills of the North Saskatchewan River Valley.

Also starting in 1908 was an electric railway that charged Edmontonians a nickel to travel on a 21 km track around their city. Edmonton was the first prairie city with a public streetcar service, and street cars could cross the High Level Bridge as of 1913. The streetcar service was disbanded in 1951.

Beginning in 1932 a motorbus system, the precursor of the modern ETS, was inaugurated. In 1978, just in advance of the Commonwealth Games, a Light Rail Transit System made its first run (at that time the third system of its kind in Canada).

Since then, the system has expanded exponentially and boasts a fleet of 49 trolleys, 219 regular buses, 536 'low floor' buses, 13 articulated buses, 29 community buses and 37 light rail vehicles.

Source: Edmonton Transit History; City of Edmonton.

Did you know...

that between 1895 and 1897, $3 million worth of gold was sifted from the North Saskatchewan River around Edmonton?

Did you know...

that the first trip by car from Edmonton to Calgary (which happened in 1906) took two days?

They Said It

"Thank God the worst of the journey is over."

**– A naive remark of a member of an English Klondike team
who believed that the journey to the Klondike from Edmonton
on the "All Canadian Route" would be a piece of cake.**

ALASKA PIPELINE

Since the start of the 20th century, the US military was concerned about the Japanese presence near Alaska. This fear increased in the spring of 1942, when Japan invaded and occupied the Aleutian islands of Kiska and Attu. Intervention seemed necessary to fend off further encroachments.

With this in mind, the American and Canadian governments collaborated on the construction of a road from Alberta to Alaska, along with a pipeline from the Norman Wells oilfield on the Mackenzie River to a refinery at Whitehorse. Edmonton became the start point and headquarters of both projects.

The building of both the pipeline and the highway involved many thousands of American servicemen and civilian contractors, all of whom came to live for a time in the small city of Edmonton. The presence of an estimated 48,000 Americans altered the complexion of the city, comprising about 10 percent of the total population. Another 25 percent of the local population found work on the projects.

All of Edmonton's office space was leased and hundreds of new homes were built near the airport. At first, Edmontonians were wary of the newcomers. But relations warmed after a blizzard brought the city to a standstill and Americans pitched in, using their construction equipment to clear roads. By October 1943, the massive construction project had ended. Edmonton, however, would never be the same.

In the late 19th century, when basketball was still in its infancy, an Edmonton team took a shining to the new sport. By capturing national and international titles, an Edmonton high school team put Edmonton on the map.

Making the story all the more amazing is the fact that these all-stars were women. Under the guidance of teacher J. Percy Page, this team of young women formed in 1912 excelled at the young sport and in 1915 won the provincial basketball championship.

All senior students in 1915, the winning women continued to play for the team after graduation, choosing as their team name, "The Edmonton Grads." For eight years, the Grads played exclusively in Alberta. In 1923 they captured the national title. Buoyed by this win, the Grads decided to take their sport to international courts, and the gamble paid off.

Between 1924 and 1946, the Grads won 27 exhibition games at Olympic Games in Paris, Amsterdam, Los Angeles and Berlin. They even beat men's teams when they lacked female opponents. The Grads also dominated the courts at home, winning the Underwood Canada-U.S. Championships from 1923 to 1940. In fact, when this series was retired, its trophy was given to the Grads for good.

In 1940, the team disbanded when its training gym was taken over for air force training during World War II. The Grads' record upon retiring was a stunning 502 wins to 20 losses.

Coach Percy Page left his Grads for Alberta politics. In 1940, he was elected as an independent to the Alberta legislature, and from 1944 to 1948 he led the provincial opposition. In 1952, by then a Progressive Conservative, Page became House Leader. In 1959 he lost his bid for reelection, but that same year was appointed Lt. Governor of Alberta, a post he held until 1966.

They Said It

"*Edmonton leads the way in all Alberta. Calgary and others follow. That is all. Goodnight.*"

– **Edmonton Mayor David Duggan, signing off from radio station CJCA on its inaugural broadcast, May 1, 1922.**

EDUCATION: THEN AND NOW

The first school opened in the area of Edmonton in 1840. This school at Fort Edmonton was short-lived and closed when the teacher returned to England. Thereafter, it was up to missionaries to operate schools for the region's children.

Public schooling was first offered in Alberta in 1881 when an Edmonton school held classes for 25 students — 22 boys and three girls. This school remained in operation until 1904.

Number of schools in 1925: 35
In 1950: 44
In 2007: 199
Number of students in 1925: 13,008
In 1950: 18,544
In 2007: 78,600

Source: Edmonton Public Schools Archives and Museum; Edmonton Public Library.

Did you know...

that it was on Christmas Day, 1894, that the first recorded hockey game was played in Edmonton?

Did you know...

that the influenza epidemic of 1918 claimed the lives of 615 Edmontonians?

OIL BOOM

On February 13, 1947, hundreds of reporters, businessmen and beaming politicians gathered on Mike Turta's farm, just south of Edmonton, to watch history unfold as the Leduc oil well (No. 1) sprung to life. After having spent $20 million on 133 failed attempts, Imperial Oil had struck black gold — and how. By the end of 1947, 147 wells had been drilled in the Leduc–Woodbend oilfield.

In the next two decades, scores of oil companies scoured the province looking for other success stories — and they found them. Oil production surged and Edmonton reaped the rewards. In 1946, the province had produced 7.7 million barrels. By 1956, this production had exploded to 143.7 million barrels and major pipelines criss-crossed the country, joining the Oil Capital of Canada to markets across the continent.

OIL BUST

The 1973 oil crisis and the Iranian Revolution of 1979 gave renewed prosperity to the city with oil prices skyrocketing worldwide. The Canadian government's National Energy Program (NEP) of 1981 retarded investment in the oil industry in Alberta. Economic losses due to NEP go as high as $100 billion. This was further compounded when world oil prices plummeted in 1986. Edmonton recovered in the mid to late-1990s, and now the city finds itself in the midst of another boom period.

RADIO

Edmonton was the first Albertan city to sign on to the airwaves. On May 1, 1922, radio station CJCA made its debut broadcast. In a battle for airwave supremacy, the following day Calgary launched its first station.

TELEPHONE TIMELINE

In 1882, Edmontonians first petitioned for phone service. When Bell Telephone turned them down — arguing that the city's population was too small — Edmontonians led by Alex Taylor took matters into their own hands and set about establishing a private phone system.

- 1884: the federal government approves $675 for the creation of an Edmonton - St. Albert line.
- 1885: the first call is made, with conversations costing fifteen cents each.
- 1888: Alex Taylor creates his own phone company with 12 phones in the city.
- 1893: Taylor's company is incorporated as the Edmonton District Telephone Company and inks a ten-year deal with the city.
- 1895: the first directory boasts 50 names.
- 1899: the city installs its first pay phone — calls cost five cents. Over 200 pay phones are operating within a year.
- 1904: Bell Canada arrives on the scene, linking Edmonton and Strathcona with Bell lines across the country while the city buys out Taylor for $17,000.
- 1908: Edmonton's public company is one of the first in Canada to introduce the automatic dial tone.
- 1990: AGT becomes Telus and five years later buys EdTel for $467 million.

Did you know...

that when Strathcona voted to amalgamate in a December 1911 plebiscite, residents of the city voted in favour of joining Edmonton by a 518 to 179 margin? Edmontonians supported the amalgamation by a 667 to 96 margin.

Weblinks

A City Called Home Stories

www.epl.ca/edmontonacitycalledhome/EPLEdmontonCityCalledRemember Type.cfm?id=Stories

Want to read first hand accounts of what it was like to live in Edmonton "back when"? Check out this collection of stories maintained by the Edmonton Public Library.

Old Strathcona Foundation

www.strathcona.org/index.html

To find out more about the Edmonton neighbourhood that was once a thriving city in its own right, visit this website about Old Strathcona. Find out what's going on in the neighbourhood, read about its history or get involved in preservation efforts.

The First People

EDMONTON'S FIRST PEOPLE

People have lived in the vicinity of Edmonton for at least 10,000 years and likely longer than that. In the historic period, the earliest people to settle the Great Plains were the Blackfoot, who moved west from the eastern Woodlands. They were probably followed by the Gros Ventre and, in the early 18th century, by the Siouian Assiniboine and then the Plains Cree. The Cree are the predominant historic group to live in the area around Edmonton.

IN A NAME

The Plains Cree are called "paskwa-wiyiniwak," which means 'plains people.' The name they call themselves is "nehiyawak," 'those who speak the same language.' They are distinguished from the more eastern relatives, the Western Woods Cree, who are called "saka-wiyiniwak," meaning 'bush people.' Although the territory of the Plains Cree was more park land than plain, their economic dependence on bison earned them the Plains designation.

RIVER PEOPLE

The Cree were divided into several groups, depending on their local.

Who are the Plains Cree?

The Plains Cree lived on the northern edge of the North American plains, in the area known as the park belt. They had occupied the area since the late 18th and early 19th centuries, when they traveled westward from east of Lake Winnipeg to pursue the fur trade, displacing several groups, including the southern Sioux, Crow and Gros Ventre, as well as the more western Blackfoot and Sarcee, as they went.

The Plains Cree emerged as a distinct group in the 1790s, and thrived with a seasonal rhythm that saw them spend summer months hunting in the woodlands to the east, and moving to the Plains in winter where the bison sustained them.

Early on, the Cree were important players in the western fur trade, acting as middlemen between European and Aboriginal fur traders. This position of prominence was abetted by the early 19th century negotiation of peace with the Blackfoot Confederacy, former trade rivals of the Cree.

Cree dominance in the western fur trade came to an end between 1790 and 1810 because they could not acquire the horses needed to partake in the bison hunt. In fact, this need for horses caused the Cree to break their truce with the Blackfoot to ally with Aboriginal groups who had greater access to the valuable creature, which led to political stability in the region.

By 1850, their partial woodland orientation had given way to life lived year round on the plains. And although still plagued by a shortage of horses, the Cree thrived, and reached their peak population of 12,500. They moved north to the Hudson's Bay Company post at Edmonton where they remained involved in the bison trade, but coped with the dwindling bison population by taking up farming and with an unsuccessful attempt to extend into Blackfoot territory.

In 1860, the Cree and Blackfoot attempted a new peace when the Cree Chief Poundmaker was adopted by the Blackfoot Chief Crowfoot. However, when the Blackfoot defeated the Cree in battle in 1871, this truce withered. At this point the Cree had little option but to take treaty to mitigate the demise of the bison and their untenable political position in the area. In 1874 the Cree at Qu'Appelle, SK, signed Treaty Four. Treaty Six, covering the Edmonton area, followed in 1876.

The River People, "cipiwiyiniwak," lived between the North Saskatchewan and Battle rivers, as far west as the border of British Columbia. They hunted westward in the vicinity of Edmonton, and south to the forks of the South Saskatchewan River.

UPSTREAM PEOPLE

The Upstream People, or "natimiwiyiniwak," the westernmost of the Cree people also lived in the vicinity of Edmonton. They traversed along the North Saskatchewan to the area now Edmonton, and south to the Battle River.

ABORIGINAL POPULATION

Nationally, 28 percent of Aboriginals live in urban centres. As of 2001, 41,000 Aboriginal people lived in Edmonton; only Winnipeg had more, with 56,000 Aboriginal people. Edmonton's Aboriginal population has grown in recent decades. Between 1981 and 2001, Edmonton's Aboriginal population mushroomed by an amazing 205 percent.

POPULATION BREAKDOWN (PERCENTAGES)

	Aboriginal	Non-Aboriginal
0-14	32.6	19.5
15-24	19.0	15.1
25-54	40.6	46.6
55-64	4.8	8.6
65+	3.1	10.3

Source: Statistics Canada.

MEDIAN AGE OF EDMONTON ABORIGINAL PEOPLE

- Total: 24.6
- Male: 22.3
- Female: 26.3

MARITAL STATUS OF EDMONTON'S ABORIGINAL PEOPLE

Of the 20,870 Aboriginals who are 15 years or older in Edmonton, the number who are:

- Single: 12,130
- Married: 4,650
- Separated: 1,425
- Divorced: 2,025
- Widowed: 640

HOUSING

Aboriginal people live in 14,250 dwellings. Of these, 4,185 are owned and 10,065 rented.

LANGUAGE

- Percentage of Edmonton Aboriginal people whose first learned language was Aboriginal and who still understand this language: 7.9
- Percentage of Aboriginal population who speak Aboriginal languages at home: 5.6
- Percentage with knowledge of Aboriginal languages: 12.2

Source: Statistics Canada.

MEDIAN INCOME OF EDMONTON ABORIGINAL PEOPLE

Aboriginal: $17,925 Non-Aboriginal: $26,026

Source: Statistics Canada.

PLAINS CREE RELIGION

The Great Creator of the Cree was known as "kicemanitow" — the entity responsible for all life. In addition the Cree, like most

Did you know...

that between 1780 and 1782 thousands of Aboriginal people on the western plains were killed by a smallpox epidemic?

Bio ALEX DECOTEAU:

ATHLETE, OFFICER, SOLDIER

On November 19, 1887, Cree Alexander Wuttunee Decoteau was born, the second youngest of five children, on the Red Pheasant Reserve near North Battleford. When Alex was just three years old, his father, Peter, was murdered, leaving Alex's mother, Mary, to raise the children.

Unable to support herself and her young family, Mary had no option but to send Alex and two siblings to the Battleford Industrial School in Saskatchewan. There, young Alex proved to be a strong student and excelled at sports — especially running.

Upon graduation, Alex moved to Edmonton, where he took up competitive running in middle and long distances. He ran his first race in May 1909 — winning a respectable second place; by that July, Alex had set a new Canadian record in a five-mile race.

Later that year, he made Canadian history yet again by joining Edmonton's police force as Canada's first Aboriginal police officer, working his way up the ranks to become Sergeant in charge of the West End Police office by 1914.

His new job did not, however, take him from his sport. In 1910, he ran in four events at the Alberta provincial championships; he won all four. And two years later, he was granted a leave of absence from work so he could represent Canada at the Stockholm Olympic Games in the 5000 m race. Despite a promising start, in mid-race Alex was stricken by leg cramps and struggled to an 8th place finish. Alex may have been disappointed, but Edmontonians were not. He arrived home to a hero's welcome.

Four years after the Olympics, Alex again offered himself for his country — this time on the battlefields of Europe. In April 1916, Alex joined the army and was deployed overseas. In the autumn of 1917 Alex was among the thousands of Canadian soldiers who fought and died at Ypres. On October 30, 1917, Alex Decoteau was felled by a German bullet. He was buried at Passchendaele. In 1985, Decoteau's friends and family gathered in Edmonton for a ceremony to bring his spirit home.

Aboriginal groups, were animistic, believing the world to be teeming with spiritual forces that they could predict and in some ways, influence. Smoking, dancing, singing, prayer and feasting all provided conduits to the spirit world.

MARRIAGE

Ideally, young people would marry within the same band. A girl's father would deliver a gift to the family of the man he wished his child to marry. If the parents of the prospective groom agreed to the match, the bride's family would build a new tepee. There, the groom would sit next to the bride and his acceptance of a gift of moccasins sealed the nuptials.

Wife exchange was also a Cree custom, and happened if a man wanted another's or if the two men were close friends. Both brides and grooms could end a marriage by returning to live with their parents, and after a time, both could remarry. The spouse who remained in the marriage tepee after the union had ended raised any children.

POLITICS

Each Plains Cree band is headed by an "okimaw," or chief. This leader — always a man — was once chosen according to his war record, wealth (displayed by his generosity) and his hunting prowess. Each band could have more than one chief — in fact, chiefs were not so much political leaders as respected men.

The Chiefship could be hereditary — often a dead chief's son took his father's place, but this was not necessarily so. After Confederation, chiefs began to be named through elections and were referred to as "akimahkan," meaning "made chief."

Each band also had two criers, elders chosen by the chief and who announced news each day.

A band council was comprised of leading men, drawn together when decisions were needed. The council worked by persuasion as each participant –starting with the youngest and ending with the most experienced — offered their positions on a given situation. When a council reached a decision, the crier broadcast it thoughout the community.

Each band also had a warrior society, complete with a unique insignia, songs and dance. Worthy men were informally chosen as warriors — called "okihcita-wak" — by male elders and most men would eventually become one. The warrior society provided for the needy and carefully guarded the bison hunt.

SUN DANCE

Perhaps the most important spiritual ceremony of the Plains Cree was the Sun Dance ceremony, or "nipakwesimowin," meaning 'thirst dance.' The ceremony was directed toward the thunder, and each ceremony was sponsored by a man who had dreamed of thunder.

The Cree believed that the Sun Dance brought long life to the sponsor, and rain to the people. The celebration of a Sun Dance was a major social event, marked by dancing, socializing, gambling and courtship. After Confederation, the Canadian government sought to stamp out the ceremony, and it was banned between 1884 and 1921.

THE SMOKING TEPEE

Known as "pihtwawikamik," this spiritual ceremony provided an opportunity for the Cree to fulfill a pledge to the spirit world, which they did by an all-night singing festival.

Typically held in the spring, the ceremony featured windigo dancers who performed a dance that stressed disorder and clowning. In Cree cosmology, the windigo is a cannibal monster, but in this dance he symbolizes not literal cannibalism, but more generally, stood for chaos.

BIRTH

Plains Cree women bore children kneeled against a support, attended by three women — a midwife who massaged and supported the labouring mom, a second midwife who cared for the newborn and a third who offered general assistance.

The baby's umbilical cord was cut and placed in an ornamental bag that the child would wear around his or her neck. The newborn was not bathed right away, but was dried off with moss, and bound in leather. A baby could not nurse for two days and, in the interim, was offered a pacifier of hard fat.

When a baby was several days old, it was placed in a leather bag, stuffed with dried moss or crumbled rotted wood — material that could be changed when it was soiled. Children were kept in moss bags until they could walk.

After a baby's birth, the parents celebrated by hosting a feast. A number of people were invited, especially old men and women known to possess supernatural powers. These men would name boy children, and old women named baby girls.

BISON

The Plains Cree and other First People of present-day Alberta were mobile people who adeptly traversed their territory hunting game, particularly bison.

Cooked meat would be boiled or fire roasted. Hides were laboriously tanned by women and then used for clothing, moccasins and tepees. Very little of the creature was wasted: tails became fly swatters, the hair was twisted into rope, teeth became jewelry, and the rough skin of the tongue made into a comb. Even bison dung was used — as a much-needed source of fuel on treeless prairies.

By the end of the 19th century, the bison were in trouble, and so were the Aboriginals who relied on them. In 1879, for the first time ever, no bison appeared on the Canadian plains.

Did you know...

that many of the First people believed that they could conjure up ghosts and spirits by whistling to the northern lights?

They Said It

> "The government has been woefully, in my view, and I would also say deliberately, violating that treaty clause."
>
> – **Native rights advocate, Willie Littlechild, on the Medicine Chest clause of Treaty Six.**

THE BISON HUNT

Before the near extinction of this mammoth mammal, the Cree hunted bison year round, moving according to the rhythms of bison migration. In summer, when the bison roamed the prairies, the Cree established large hunting camps and dispatched a party to locate the animals. Once located, hunters, both mounted and on foot, pursued the herd, focusing on one bison at a time.

Where possible, bison herds were corralled to a location where they would founder, such as a marsh or over a steep bank. In winter, as herds entered northern woodlands, the Cree would trap the animals in pounds. The construction of pounds was supervised by shamans whose spiritual powers benefited the site.

A spherical area of 30 to 40 feet was cleared and brush and logs assembled into a wall ten to fifteen feet tall. A runway was built leading up to the pound, making a sharp turn at its entrance. As bison approached, mounted hunters herded them into the pound, confining them for an easy kill.

ORIGINS OF TREATY SIX

Aboriginal people living on what would become the Canadian plains, including the vicinity of Edmonton were, by the 1870s, facing hardship and uncertainty. The bison were disappearing at an alarming rate and they were ravaged by a smallpox epidemic. Meanwhile, European interest in western lands was piqued.

In 1867, the newly Confederated Canada pledged its intent to include western territories in its union. All too aware of Euro-Canadians' interest in their land, Aboriginal chiefs living in the vicinity of Edmonton knew they had to do something to save their people from these ominous circumstances. The negotiation of a treaty (like those already negotiated in the east) with the Canadian government seemed the best hope and many Cree pressed Ottawa to make a treaty.

From Ottawa's perspective, treaties promised a way of peaceably settling western lands that were coveted by settlers and Canadian nation builders. And so, in the summer of 1876, Treaty Six was signed. The majority of Aboriginal signatories were Plains Cree, although bands of Woodland Cree were also represented.

TREATY SIX

In the 19th century, the Canadian government signed a series of numbered treaties with Aboriginal people. Edmonton is located in the territory covered by Treaty Six which stretches from Edmonton to Red Deer and across the border into Saskatchewan. Signed in 1876, this is one of three Alberta numbered treaties (the others being seven and eight). In all, 16 First Nations live in territory bound by Treaty Six; most are Plains Cree.

Under the terms of the treaty, each Aboriginal family of five received 2.5 km^2 of land. In addition, people in treaty bands were provided a one-time cash payment of $12 plus an annual annuity of five dollars. Chiefs were to receive a horse and cart or wagon, and bands were promised $1,500 annually for ammunition and fishing twine, provisions in times of famine, and a medicine chest, to be housed in the home of the Indian Agent.

In 1993, the office of the Confederacy of Treaty Six First Nations was created to provide a united political voice for Treaty Six First Nations, a voice Aboriginals believe is needed to protect the treaty rights of all First People.

Did you know...

that it was not until 1960 that Ottawa gave First Nations people with treaty status the right to vote? Seven years later, Albertans with treaty status voted in their first provincial election.

OPPOSITION TO TREATY SIX

Not everyone approved of Treaty Six. At meetings held in August of 1876 in advance of the negotiations, chiefs debated the issue. Later that month when the much-respected Mistahimusqua (Big Bear) arrived at Fort Pitt, he was dismayed to discover that chiefs there had already agreed to the terms. Distrusting the government negotiators and opposed to Treaty terms that bound the Cree to a foreign Canadian law, Mistahimusqua opposed the agreement. For six years, he refused to sign the treaty and lobbied for it to be revised. Only in 1882, his peopled felled by starvation and disease in the wake of depleted bison herds, did Mistahimusqua reluctantly endorse the agreement.

MEDICINE CHEST

One of the most important terms of Treaty Six is its provision of a "medicine chest" for bands bound by the agreement. The treaty specified that "a medicine chest shall be kept at the house of each Indian Agent for the use and benefit of the Indians at the direction of such agent."

In the years since the treaty's signing, this clause has been widely disputed. First Nations people insist that this treaty clause guarantees them full and complete federally-funded healthcare. The federal government, however, has downplayed its health care obligations, interpreting the medicine chest clause narrowly, as a promise to literally furnish a sort of first aid kit for Treaty Six signatories.

Convinced that the spirit of the treaty requires Ottawa to allocate full healthcare as a treaty right, Aboriginal people have taken this issue to court.

In 1935, a Saskatchewan Court ruling, Dreaver et al. v. The King, Ottawa's responsibility was narrowly defined to mean medicines and health supplies, not full healthcare services. Thirty years later, another provincial case, Regina v. Johnston upheld the Aboriginal perspective that the medicine chest clause meant that Treaty Six First Nations are entitled by receive complete health care services.

To date, however, the issue remains unresolved and has still not been heard by the Supreme Court of Canada. Although the Canadian federal government pays for most Aboriginal health care, it refuses to acknowledge that this is a treaty right of Treaty Six First Nations.

Bio JANE ASH POITRAS

Widely recognized as a world famous painter and printmaker, Cree artist Jane Ash Poitras enlivens Edmonton's art scene. Her mixed media canvases and prints are wildly expressive collages of Aboriginal imagery and fields of colour inspired by the likes of Wassily Kandinsky and Hans Kofman.

A graduate of the prestigious Columbia University in New York, she has lectured at post-secondary schools through North America and Europe on shamanic and contemporary Native art. Her work has been displayed in the National Gallery of Canada, the Canadian Museum of Civilization and the Brooklyn Museum in New York.

Poitras has also kept her art grounded, unpretentiously public and close to home. In 2005, at a park near her central Edmonton home, she erected a monument to Ojibwa artist Carl Beam made of bison skulls, fake moose legs, boulders and an eagle feather. Neighbours didn't appreciate the aesthetic and city officials tore it down.

City council encouraged Poitras to get involved in public art projects, but she declined, saying, "You'd have to go through five bureaucrats and have to do this and that. That's not the way you tell an artist to make art." On another occasion Poitras painted the license plates of johns cruising her neighbourhood for prostitutes, after being harassed herself while out walking with her infant daughter.

Poitras was born in Fort Chipewyan but was placed in foster care at a young age with an elderly devout Catholic woman in Edmonton named Margeurite Runck. Poitras thus grew up in a highly spiritual home, but one that was entirely divorced from her Cree heritage. She only completed a fine arts degree at the University of Alberta in 1983 after first getting a "practical" education in microbiology.

They Said It

"We need to do something to bring down these barriers. The way you start to correct historical injustices is to give people a place to come talk about the issues."

– Aboriginal consultant Lewis Cardinal, of the city of Edmonton's 2004 creation of the Edmonton Urban Aboriginal Accord Initiative

WHITE AND A RED PAPER

The 1960s began with optimism for Natives in Alberta. As the North American civil rights movement gathered steam, the "Red Power" movement asserted Natives' political, territorial and cultural rights, challenged oppressive laws to which they were subject and demanded that the Canadian Department of Indian Affairs and Northern Development (DIAND) be replaced with self-government and meaningful Native control of Native lands and resources.

It was in this climate that the Liberal government of Pierre Elliott Trudeau decided to overhaul the Indian Act. In 1968, Trudeau's Minister of Indian Affairs, a young Jean Chrétien, met with Native communities across Canada where he learned that Natives were most concerned with land claim and treaty rights recognition and an assurance of Native peoples' special status in Canada.

By June 1969, Ottawa's Indian Act revisions were complete and Native leaders were flown to Ottawa for the new Act's unveiling. On June 25th, Native leaders listened from the House of Commons Gallery as Chrétien delivered the now infamous White Paper on Indian Policy. Just ten pages long, the White Paper made some stunning recommendations that clearly ignored Native wishes. Without addressing the concerns raised in consultations, the White Paper called for the Indian Act to be repealed, for treaties to be terminated and for the DIAND to be eliminated.

Natives were outraged and united in their opposition and it was the Edmonton-based Alberta Indian Association (AIA) that penned the official Native response to Ottawa's proposal. Titled Citizens Plus, the Red Paper insisted that Natives' special status continue and that rather than abolish the Indian Act, a new one should be written and a new federal agency — one devoted it its moral and legal obligations — be created. The Red Paper insisted that Ottawa recognize treaty and aboriginal rights and, above all, insisted that the offensive White Paper not be implemented. Facing such vehement and widespread opposition, the federal government retracted the White Paper in 1971.

AT HOME IN EDMONTON?

Despite the creation in 2004 of the Edmonton Urban Aboriginal Accord Initiative, a program aimed at improving the lives of Edmonton's Aboriginal population, there are signs that Aboriginals are less than satisfied with life in the city.

In March 2006, the city's Aboriginal Urban Affairs Committee undertook a dialogue with nearly 2,000 of the city's Aboriginal residents. The discussions revealed that Edmonton's Aboriginal people were concerned about deficient housing, a lack of respect shown to their culture and language and insufficient employment and educational options.

As well, in a survey of 500 Aboriginal Edmontonians, a third of respondents disagreed with the statement that that Edmonton was welcoming city for Aboriginals; another 11 percent "strongly" disagreed with this idea.

They Said It

"The American Indians had their heroes. We didn't have many of them and Alex is surely one of them. He accomplished more in 30 years than many of us will in a lifetime."

— Gerald Wuttunee, Decoteau relative

Weblinks

Edmonton Aboriginal Urban Affairs Committee

www.aboriginal-edmonton.com/committee.htm

Check out this website of this volunteer committee of the Edmonton City Council. The site, which offers information about and for Aboriginal people living in Edmonton, has a mandate to "promote the awareness and development of all Aboriginal people in the city of Edmonton."

Treaty 6

www.ainc-inac.gc.ca/pr/trts/trty6_e.html

Read Treaty 6 for yourself at this site, maintained by Indian and Northern Affairs Canada.

www.albertasource.ca/treaty6/

To find about more about Treaty 6 — its origin, making and contemporary implications — visit this web site that is part of the Alberta Online Encyclopedia.

The Plains Cree: An Ethnographic, Historical and Comparative Study

www.schoolnet.ca/autochtone/Plains_Cree/index-e.html

Although it is dated (it was first published in 1936) this classic study of Plains Cree ethnology by David G. Manelbaum offers wide ranging information on Cree culture, albeit through the eyes of a non-Native male at the start of the last century.

Go Ahead, Take Five More

As you can probably tell, we are partial to things you can count on one hand. This chapter is just more of that. It is designed to be fun, entertaining and insightful, not only in details about the city, but also about the person making the choices. It is a chapter that could have continued beyond the bounds of this book. Edmontonians, famous and not so famous, were literally bursting at the seams with opinions about their city.

TAKE 5: JASON SMITH'S TOP FIVE BATTLE OF ALBERTA MOMENTS

It seems that the rivalry between Alberta's largest cities knows no bounds. It is contested on numerous fronts from backrooms, legislative floors and especially from football fields and hockey arenas. Jason Smith may be an Oiler captain but he is a Calgary boy. After stints with the New Jersey Devils and Toronto Maple Leafs, Calgary's Smith was traded in 1999 to the rivals at the north end of Highway 2. Until the Oilers traded him in 2007 he was warrior in many Battles of Alberta. Here are his picks for one of the most hotly contested rivalries in sport.

1. Theoren Fleury's goal celebration against the Edmonton Oilers in the 1991 playoffs.

2. Wayne Gretzky's slapshot over the shoulder of Mike Vernon in the 1988 playoffs.

3. Doug Flutie and the Calgary Stampeders comeback against the Edmonton Eskimos in the 1992 Western Final. Doug Flutie scores from the one-yard line and his shoe goes flying in the air.

4. Edmonton Eskimos Western Final victory over the Calgary Stampeders in Calgary in 1996. The weather was so awful, it had to be -25 with wind down on the field.

5. The Battle of Alberta never ends. Calgary and Edmonton play eight times each season and it's a battle each time.

TAKE 5: GILBERT BOUCHARD'S TOP 5 MUST-VISIT DINING LOCALES

It's no secret that when CBC personality and Edmonton Journal writer Gilbert Bouchard isn't talking about Edmonton's arts scene, he's telling some-one about the best places to eat. It's been a while since he's been in the restaurant reviewing game, but he's still got the chops. The following is his take on a handful of eateries that are part of this city's culinary history as one eats one's way through the good, the bad and the just plain ugly.

1) **Motoraunt (12406-66 St.):** Let's start with the ugly. This odd-ball eatery may look like it was dropped nastily onto its lot, having been built in a jury-rigged fashioned around an old double-decker bus, but much to the ire of municipal rule makers and NIMBY types, the burgers and fries served up here are as divine as the restaurant itself is aesthetically unpleasing. Also, the joint boasts some of the largest serving sizes in town (i.e., how many others serve a burger that feeds four?), so don't come a knocking at this rocking bus unless you're willing to pound it back.

2) Barb & Ernie's Restaurant (9906 72 Ave.): This is another joint that isn't shy about the portions, delicate eating habits and/or a quiet dining environment. One of Edmonton's most long-lived eateries, most famous for its humongous breakfasts and outrageous options, this German eatery became an institution as much for its hard-core Albertan plain-talking and friendly ways as its food. You're not just eating the best truck stop omelet you've ever had at Barb & Ernie's, you're eating a big slice of Alberta culinary history.

3) Bistro Praha Gourmet Café (10168 100A St.): Speaking of history, the Bistro Praha has got to be one of Edmonton's oldest and longest-lived European bistros and one of the grandfathers of the city's coffeehouse trade. A virtual oasis of dining pleasure back in the early 80s when Edmonton's downtown was way less hopping than it is now, the Bistro may not be the last word in trendsters' hangouts in the 21st century, but it still offers up a civilized atmosphere (yes, a bit worse for the wear) and a darn tasty array of continental delights.

4) Café Select (10018 106 St.) and/or Dadeo (10548a Whyte Ave.): These two unrelated restaurants are only being grouped together for effect: both historically well-run and well-designed eateries, they are also the yesterday and the today of dining hipness. Just as Select, still a popular and tasty dining option in 2007, was THE place to be seen in the early 80s by the movers and shakers, Dadeo is where the cool crowd of Old Strathcona gather to nosh and to be seen. Points can and will be made by members of old and new guard if invitations are tendered to either place and the names of chefs and/or owners can be dropped in conversation (or at reservation time) or into a well-crafted "I-was-there-when" anecdote.

5) **Unheard of Restaurant (9602 82 Ave.):** As the name implies, this exquisite little eatery nestled at the uncool end of Whyte Avenue near the Mill Creek Ravine is both a culinary delight and not exactly a household name. Famous for its profoundly sedate and civilized atmosphere as well as a sophisticated and deft menu, this restaurant is a rare gem in an eating out universe boasting more rhinestones than genuine sparklers. Eat here once and you'll be torn as to whether you should brag ceaselessly about your time here, or keep it your neat little secret.

TAKE 5: DARYL BENSON'S TOP FIVE PHOTOGENIC SPOTS IN EDMONTON

Daryl Benson is a photographer/writer born and raised in Edmonton. He has self-published two books, *A Guide to Photographing the Canadian Landscape* and *Alberta Images*. He writes for *Photo Life*, *Outdoor Photographer* and *PC Photo Magazines* and shoots stock for Masterfile and Getty.

1. **The Entire Edmonton River Valley** is among the most beautiful green spaces of any Canadian city. A favourite view of the river and city skyline is from the south end of Forest Heights Park.

2. **Muttart Conservatory**, especially at Christmas when the pyramids are trimmed in lights and hundreds of Poinsettias fill the pavilions.

3. **Fort Edmonton Park** is a great historical location. Beautiful in early autumn and during the Harvest Festival held in late August. Stop by the John Jansen Nature Centre too—it's right next door.

4. **Alberta Legislative Grounds**, beautiful in the summer, but also nice at Christmas when all the trees are trimmed in lights.

5. **Queen Elizabeth Park** is in the Edmonton River Valley, with beau-

tiful surroundings and backdrops. It's a favourite spot to photograph in autumn and is usually not crowded. The exception is during the spring/summer wedding season when many portrait and wedding photographers take advantage of its many natural settings.

TAKE 5: PAULA SIMONS' FIVE FAVOURITE EDMONTON-AREA DAYTRIPS

Paula Simons is the *Edmonton Journal*'s popular and provocative city columnist. A born-and-bred Edmontonian, whose family roots in the city go back more than 100 years, Simons is a graduate of the University of Alberta, Stanford University and the Poynter Institute for Media Studies. Her many honours include three National Newspaper Award citations of merit, for excellence in editorial writing column writing, and political reporting. Simons does her daytripping in the company of her husband David, her daughter Celia, and their bichon frise, Echo.

1. **The Ukrainian Cultural Heritage Village** is only a 40 minute drive from downtown Edmonton, but a day trip to the park lets you travel back in time a hundred years to the days when Ukrainian pioneers were breaking land and building homesteads in northeastern Alberta. It comes complete with an authentic train station, hotel, blacksmith shop, one-room school house, and a fully-functioning grain elevator. But I love the village most because the talented young actors who play the parts of the frontier community stay so fiercely in character. Each person assumes the role of a real Alberta pioneer, and brings that individual back to life with delightful zest and integrity. It's not just a heritage museum — its a chance to immerse yourself in a great piece of improvisational theatre.

2. **Devonian Botanic Gardens**. You couldn't ask for a more tranquil get-away than a day trip to the Devonian Botanic Gardens. The 80-acre facility, operated by the University of Alberta, is a horticultural

research centre as well as a stunning public park. There's an alpine garden, a native people's garden, a wonderful sensory garden where you can touch and smell and even taste the flowers, and an indoor butterfly pavilion, where you can walk through a tropical jungle while butterflies flit past or even land on your shoulder. The Devonian's crown jewel is the stunning Kurimoto Japanese Garden, an authentic zen-style garden complete with waterfall and pagodas.

3. **Lacombe** is one of Alberta's more charming towns. A hundred years ago, Lacombe was a major commercial centre, but World War I plunged the town into a recession from which it never really recovered. The result is that Lacombe's old main street has one of the finest collections of Edwardian-era brick buildings in the province, and decade ago the town had the foresight to restore the main street to its 1907 glory. It's now one of the prettiest heritage streetscapes in Alberta, complete with a blacksmithing museum and an historic interpretive centre. What I love best about Lacombe is its famous Friday farmer's market. You'll find no fresher tomatoes, cucumbers, beans or peppers anywhere.

4. **Bon Accord** is home to two of my favourite farmers. Tam Andersen runs Prairie Gardens where you can buy great bedding plants or pick your own peas and strawberries and pumpkins. In recent years, she's expanded to include a petting farm, a devilishly difficult corn mazeand a wide variety of weekend festivals. The Fairy Berry Festival, on the August long-weekend, includes fairies, pirates, face-painting, wagon rides, kids' games and a delicious wealth of strawberry desserts and delicacies. All through October, Prairie Gardens runs its Haunted Pumpkin Festival, complete with haunted houses and pumpkin pies. Up the road is Lola Canola, aka Patti Milligan, a local beekeeper who does live bee demonstrations and gives guests the chance to harvest their own honey or do beeswax crafts.

5. **The David Thompson Highway**. Sometimes, it's not about the destination, it's about the journey. Highway 11, the David Thompson Highway, gets my vote as the most beautiful drive in Alberta. And in this Rocky Mountain province, that's saying something. The David Thompson, which connects Red Deer and Rocky Mountain House to the Jasper-Banff Highway, is the road less travelled, an almost secret bypass through rolling foothills, improbably beautiful lakes and rugged mountains. Where other mountain highways clog up with RVs and minivans, you can drive the David Thompson and feel as if you're all alone in the wilderness. Abraham Lake, below Mt. Michener, may be artificial — it's the byproduct of the Big Horn Dam — but its teal-green water, often topped with whitecaps, is one of central Alberta's true wonders.

TAKE 5: DR. INDIRA SAMARASEKERA'S
TOP FIVE ISSUES FACING UNIVERSITIES

Dr. Indira Samarasekera is the 12th President and Vice-Chancellor of the University of Alberta, one of Canada's most respected research-intensive universities. Since taking office in July 2005, she has spearheaded the development of "Dare to Discover: A Vision for a Great University," a seminal document that will serve as the guiding force in the University's quest to become one of the top 20 universities in the world by 2020.

1. **Provision of an international education for students** to enhance the global perspective and intercultural climate of the university and provide students with quality opportunities to develop the knowledge, skills and perspectives required to live and work in the changing international environment of the twenty-first century.

2. **Delivery of world-class education** to increase the support and funding for learning, research and discovery, focusing on investments to build world-class excellence in competitive areas.

3. **Cultivation of differentiation among universities** to differentiate between highly research-intensive universities and universities that concentrate on providing a liberal arts education. Canada needs to work hard at encouraging greater differentiation among its universities, allowing some universities to excel in specialized areas and offer the best education and research opportunities in the world.

4. **Improvement of access to university for all students** to prepare our society to support a knowledge economy, and ensure high quality learning is accessible to all individuals and communities.

5. **Increase of the number of graduate students.** Graduate students deliver knowledge to business and society through knowledge transfer and commercialization. Their discoveries are invaluable to an innovative, progressive and vibrant economy.

TAKE 5: MARIE GYNANE-WILLIS'
FIVE FABULOUS EDMONTONIAN PLAYWRIGHTS

Marie Gynane-Willis is executive director of Theatre Alberta, the Provincial Arts Service Organization for theatre. Gynane-Willis has worked in the Alberta arts community as an administrator, programmer and educator, and is a graduate of the University of Alberta and The Drama Centre, London, England. She was coerced into choosing just five playwrights and warns there are many more deserving praise.

1. **Vern Thiessen.** "Einstein's Gift" premiered at the Citadel Theatre in 2003 and won the Governor General's Literary Award for Drama that same year. The play had its American premiere, running off broadway at the Epic Theatre Centre in NYC, in 2005. Other favourites include "Shakespeare's Will," "Apple" and "Blowfish."

2. **David Belke.** A Fringe Festival favourite, resident playwright at Shadow Theatre and cast member of weekly live improvised soap opera Die-Nasty, David has been published by Samuel French ("Blackpool and Parrish" and "That Darn Plot") and had his plays produced in Canada, the US, England and Northern Ireland.

3. **Conni Massing.** Conni divides her time between writing for theatre, film and television. Her murder mystery "The Aberhart Summer" (Alberta Theatre Projects and the Citadel Theatre) captures the essence of Alberta in the Dirty '30s during the Social Credit Movement and "Bible Bill" Aberhart's reign as Premier.

4. **Stewart Lemoine.** Stewart writes almost exclusively for his company, Teatro La Quindicina. His plays are typically populated by Edmonton's best comedic talent and have been described as "Canadian Comedy of Manners." "Pith!" was awarded the New York International Fringe's Award for Overall Excellence in Playwriting in 2004.

5. **Mieko Ouchi.** In addition to being a Co-Artistic Director at Concrete Theatre, Edmonton's Theatre for Young Audiences, Mieko also writes sweeping historical epics, à la "The Blue Light" and "The Red Priest (Eight Ways To Say Goodbye)" — both produced by Workshop West Playwrights' Theatre and ATP in Calgary. She is making her mark on the Canadian theatre scene as an advocate for strong women.

TAKE 5: JIM HOLE'S
TOP FIVE QUIRKY PLANTS THAT GROW IN EDMONTON

Born and raised in the Edmonton area, Jim Hole is the co-owner of Hole's Greenhouses and Gardens Ltd. in St. Albert, Alberta. He graduated from the University of Alberta with a BSc in agriculture and is currently the Honourary Co-chair of Centenary Celebrations for the University of Alberta. Jim is a contributor to the *Edmonton Journal* and is the co-author, author or editor of 11 gardening books. When he's not busy writing, Jim appears regularly on CBC Radio Edmonton and on CBC's Wildrose Country. As Hole notes: "Plants are endlessly fascinating and some are downright strange." Here is his top five list of quirky plants that grow in Edmonton:

1. **Pitcher plant** (*Sarracenia purpurea*)
It grows in boggy areas around Edmonton and is carnivorous, feasting from time to time on a variety of insects.

2. **Jack-in-the-pulpit** (*Arisaema triphyllum*)
It is a transgendered plant, meaning it is capable of changing genders depending on the suitability of its growing environment.

3. **Indian Pipe** (*Monotropa uniflora*)
This plant is ghostly white and is one of the few plants in the world that does not require sunlight. It has no chlorophyll and, much like a mushroom, derives its energy from decomposing organic material in the soil.

4. **Dwarf Mistletoe** (*Arceuthobium americanum*)
This parasitic plant attacks the trunks and branches of trees in the pine family, causing the trees to grow in a distorted fashion. It's mature seeds 'explode' off the plant.

5. **Gas Plant** (*Dictamnus albus v. purpureus*)
This plant gives off a combustible gas when the conditions are just right. Holding a match near a bloom on a warm, humid, calm evening can cause the gas to ignite with an audible pop.

TAKE 5: TODD BABIAK'S
TOP FIVE "LITERARY" SPOTS IN EDMONTON

Todd Babiak has published two novels, *The Garneau Block*, which was nominated for the Giller Prize, and *Choke Hold*. His third novel, *The Book of Stanley*, will be published by McClelland and Stewart in the fall of 2007. He is the culture columnist at the *Edmonton Journal* and appears on several "top five people who should be stabbed" lists. (www.toddbabiak.com) The following is his authoritative, non-exhaustive list of literary spots in Edmonton, as drawn from novels, short stories and a number of unpublished poems by undergraduates at the University of Alberta.

1. **The High Level Bridge** – All discerning suicides consider the High Level Bridge first, before moving on to other locations like the top of Manulife Place or the man-made swamp in Hawrelak Park.

2. **The Hotel Macdonald** – Like most Western Canadian cities, Edmonton is short on Victorian architecture and old money. The Hotel Macdonald, now a Saudi-owned Fairmont, supplies the illusion of grandeur. Of special note is the Confederation Lounge, one of the best hotel bars in the country. Canadian political science buffs love to play "Name That Father of Confederation" under the art and tapestries.

3. **The North Saskatchewan River** – Deep, haunting and murky, the river holds special mysteries. Revered by our noble First Nations Peoples and by summertime patio dwellers alike, the river is both beautiful and dangerous. Much of Edmonton's most expensive real estate lies next to it, or on its banks, despite the danger of stinky flooding.

4. **Whyte Avenue** – Once the main street of Strathcona, Whyte Avenue is Edmonton's southside rival for downtown and is the city's bloodstream, literally and figuratively. On weekend nights, the pot-pourri and yoga boulevard becomes a giant unlicensed no-rules fighting pit for young men from the suburbs.

5. **Jasper and 101st** – This is where old meets new, where Starbucks meets empty office space, where meth addicts and homeless people wander among men and women in $2,500 suits. See that Hummer in the loading zone, parked next to the abandoned 1989 Tempo with Ontario plates? Welcome to the heart of Edmonton.

TAKE 5: MICHAEL WALTERS'
FIVE FAVOURITE NEIGHBOURHOOD REJUVENATIONS

Michael Walters is a writer and community organizer living in South Edmonton. He is married to Kara and has two young sons, Isaac and Samson.

1. **Norwood** – This is a neighbourhood that is patient in its rebirth, and bold in the face of attack after attack from slum lords, prostitution and do gooders. It is slowly becoming a multi-cultural business district.

2. **Highlands** – Much like Norwood, but with less crime and decay, Highlands exemplifies some of the greatest community leadership in Edmonton. There are healthy pockets of small family-owned businesses and active schools and community leagues and some of Edmonton's most beautiful housing.

3. **Greisbach** – As far as new neighbourhoods go, Greisbach is the smartest in Edmonton. Dubbed an Urban Village, Greisbach is built with community in mind. It is only minutes from downtown.

4. **Crestwood** – How do you get people out of their cars and onto the sidewalks? Give them something to walk to. A bakery, a burger joint, a wine bar, clothing shops, medical facilities, it's all there in the new Crestwood, which is really the old Crestwood off 149th street, but with a cool market hub stuck right in the middle.

5. **Ascot Gardens in Wellington** – an innovative developer will turn 200 sad looking flat top inefficient town homes into 750 modern energy efficient condos. The greatest part about this high density, low impact development is the commitment to affordable housing, agreed to by the developer and the old tenants of the old townhouses, so no displacement will occur and the city will have an integrated affordable housing model to boot.

TAKE 5: CHERYL MAHAFFY'S FIVE BEST KEPT EDMONTON SECRETS

A transplant from Minnesota, Cheryl Mahaffy co-authored *Agora Borealis: Engaging in Sustainable Architecture* and appears in the anthologies *100 Journeys*, *Big Enough Dreams*, *Edmonton on Location* and *Outside of Ordinary*. She interned at the *Wall Street Journal* while earning an M.A. in journalism from Indiana University, and worked at Minnesota's award-winning *Northfield News* before moving to Edmonton in 1981.

Drop in on her home office in the Highlands, and you might find her at work on a magazine article or cajoling neighbours to contribute to the community newsletter. She is also unearthing stories of women architects for a project entitled *Women Building Alberta*. The Rocky Mountains figure large in the Mahaffy family's leisure time. In winter, it's screaming down mountain paths on cross-country skis. In summer, the menu shifts to hiking, both here and around the globe.

1. **Highlands shopping district.** "Meet me at Mandolin." It's a favourite phrase at our house. After coffee and a browse at Mandolin Books & Coffee Company (6419 112 Avenue), smarten up your home with finds from one-of-a-kind shops. Then repair to either of the street's two fine eateries, La Boheme (French) or Bacon (vegetarian with a twist).

2. **Railway bike trails.** Boom-city traffic got you down? Psst, here's a secret: Use the trails. You'll avoid crowds, minimize the lights and get where you're going in a flash. Thanks to a newish trail alongside the LRT tracks, coupled with the Railtown bikeway, I can finally bike across the river to the University of Alberta without breaking into (much of) a sweat.

3. **The King's University College.** Students from around the world pilgrimage to 9125 50 Street to study with renowned music faculty, soak up a liberal arts education in intimate classrooms and do undergraduate research with scientists who are authoring some of tomorrow's textbooks. Yet herds of Edmontonians march off to classrooms where the body count numbers in the hundreds. Another home-town prophet looking for an audience, perhaps?

4. **Cityfarm Edmonton.** Once upon a time just a few years ago, this unique playground overlooking the North Saskatchewan River sprouted from the fertile minds of folks who want to help Edmontonians stay connected to the land. Here kids and the young at heart can cook bannock in a clay oven, gather eggs warm from the nest, build all sorts of things and grow their own lunch. Cityfarm is located at Riverbend Gardens, one of several fertile farms within city limits that may be preserved as part of a proposed Northeast Green Zone.

5. **The Carrot Community Arts Coffeehouse.** The name's quite a mouthful, and no wonder. Here's a spot that puts mouths in action— eating, drinking, singing, telling tales, digesting art and just chewing the fat. You'll find Carrot at 9351 118 Avenue, along a segment of Alberta Avenue that is reviving through concerted grassroot effort. Why Carrot? Think Paul Cezanne: "The day is coming when a single carrot, freshly observed, will set off a revolution."